W9-BWL-021

FIGURE *it* OUT

**Making Smart Decisions in
a Dumbed-Down World**

Robert W. Wendover

ARTICULATE PUBLICATIONS

Copyright © 2014 by Robert W. Wendover. All rights reserved. Printed in the United States of America. Except as permitted under the United States Copyright Act of 1976, no part of this publication may be reproduced or distributed in any form or by any means stored in a database or retrieval system without the prior written permission of the publisher.

ISBN: 978-0-9848040-5-4
Library of Congress Control Number: 2013912803

Book design by Glen M. Edelstein

This book is available at special quantity discounts to use as premiums and sales promotions or for use in corporate training programs. To obtain additional information, please e-mail us at bulksales@articulatepublications.
This book is printed on acid-free paper.

FIGURE *it* OUT

To Wendy, Erin and Katie, the biggest blessings in my life

CONTENTS

USING QR CODES TO GET MORE OUT OF THIS BOOK

Use the QR, or quick response, codes at the beginning of every chapter to get more out of this book. *Figure It Out!* is all about how to make smart decisions in our dumbed-down world. QR codes have allowed me to add more than 70 minutes of video content to what you will read on these pages. You, the reader, will learn best when you interact with the ideas I present rather just scanning the words and watching the videos. So each chapter-related clip will challenge you to put the principles into action. After all, the best way to learn something is to *do* it. Periodically, I will add additional content, including interviews with those who model this book's principles.

There are two options for activating them:

1. If you are using an iPhone, iPad, MacBook, or other Apple device, download the QR Reader from the Apple Store.

2. If you are using a smart phone with Android software, download the QR Reader from the Android Marketplace. Just search for "QR Reader."

When you scan the code at the beginning of each chapter, you will be automatically connected to the corresponding video segment, seventeen in all. Take advantage of the interactivity of this technology to enhance your ability to make smart decisions. Now, on with the book!

"No one teaches us how to figure stuff out. We've always learned best from mistakes. So what is the escape key doing to us?"

INTRODUCTION

Simpler Answers and Harder Decisions

Decisions. We all make lots of them every day. Most are pretty easy. Some are harder. Then there are those that are downright difficult. Decisions in general are getting more complicated. Technology was supposed to make them easier, but it hasn't. The number of choices we have for everything has exploded. There's more pressure to make decisions than ever before. At the same time, the stakes seem to be higher for any significant commitment.

So what can you do to become a smarter decision

maker? That's what this book is all about. People make decisions for one of two reasons: To gain pleasure or avoid pain. Being a smart decision maker means you set aside emotion and think tactically. The bigger the issue the more you need to do this.

HOW THIS BOOK IS DESIGNED

Each chapter contains a "chapter before the chapter," just like this one. It will cover the important points and summarize the takeaways. You'll also find questions throughout the book to get you thinking. (What better time to work on your decision making than while reading a book on decision making?) Finally, there is a QR code at the beginning of each chapter that will link you to additional video insights about that particular topic. (If you don't know how to use QR codes, there's an explanation on page ix.)

"Figure it out" is not a strategy. It is a mindset! Smart decision makers embrace the principles on these pages. Let's get started.

Decision making. . . it's something we do every day, right? Got a situation at work? We figure it out. Got a problem at home? We fix it. Have an issue with a neighbor? We solve it.

Only it's not that easy, is it? Lots of stuff doesn't turn out as planned. We *think* we know what to do. Then it doesn't work. We try to come up with a solution. But there doesn't seem to be a right answer. We get started and realize we don't really understand the problem. Then there are times when we don't know where to begin.

Take Mike for example. He's new to his job. He's been through the training. He's been assigned some tasks. He knows what he's supposed to do. Someone explained the steps. It seemed easy enough. But watching it being done and doing it are two different things. He has to make some judgments. He has to decide on his own. He's responsible. Others are depending on him.

Then his mind fills with ideas of what can go wrong. He could make mistakes. He could solve the wrong problems. He could cost the company money. He might be embarrassed. If he screws up, others might not trust him. People might laugh. He might get fired! Maybe if he doesn't do anything, no one will notice. Have you ever felt like Mike?

There's Yvonne. She's a military spouse whose husband is deployed overseas. She juggles a part-time job at the school with raising two young boys. She runs the household and manages family finances. She's in charge of home maintenance, auto repair, and everything else.

Last week the garage roof started to leak. Now there's water pooling on the floor under the car. The two people she called for repairs gave outrageous estimates. Have you ever felt like Yvonne?

Finally, there's Albert. He's always been the computer whiz. Ask him a question about hardware or software and he's got a solution. Have a problem on any topic and he'll send you a link. But last month, he was put in charge of a group of volunteers at the local community center. Over the past few weeks, he's discovered that managing people is different than managing computers. With computers, what you see is what you get. With people, you don't get anything of the sort. They don't show up for assignments. They *say* they will do something and they *don't*. They ask questions rather than figuring out things for themselves.

Then there are the personalities. Some think they know it all. Others are simply showing up to fulfill a school requirement. Still others just talk and talk and talk. On top of this, Albert can't search for a solution online. It's not like he can Google, "fixing people problems." He knows that sounds funny. But he's realizing how much he's grown to depend on the web for answers to everything. Have you felt like Albert?

HOW DOES THIS RELATE TO YOU?

Chances are, you can make a list of other situations like the ones facing Mike, Yvonne, and Albert. There are so many around. You might identify with these three because you've been there. Let's face it, life is getting more complicated. Marketers keep telling us that our lives are getting easier and more convenient. None of us believe it for a second. Computers are supposed to save time and effort. All these apps are supposed to make our decisions easier. If only that were true!

The bottom line? It's getting tougher to make smart decisions. Some of this has to do with how busy we are. Some of it has to do with too many distractions. Some of it has to do with too much information. Some of it has to do with too many people trying to give us too many options that serve *their* purposes, not ours.

It's not that we're getting stupid. It's not that we're getting lazy. It's just that we're increasingly manipulated by the people and systems around us. Sure, you think you know what to do, but the website doesn't provide that option. Yes, you'd like to noodle the problem through, but the boss says, "Get it done. Don't take time to think!" Sure, you'd like to look at the bigger picture, but with all the decisions to be made every day, you just get tired of thinking.

You might be irritated by Mike's, Yvonne's, and Albert's hesitancy about making decisions. You may have come of age at a time when, if you asked for help, people said "Figure it out!" It's not that they didn't want to be helpful. They just had more faith in you to solve the problem than you had in yourself. You struggled a bit. You solved the problem. You came out the other end with a boost in your confidence.

Now you watch people grow more and more dependent on outside cues and instructions. "They need to develop self-reliance!" you think. You're tempted to say something like, "Get over yourself! Take a shot! Noodle your way through! Nothing's that hard! We've all been through it."

Frankly, you probably feel some empathy *and* some irritation for these people. Problems come in all shapes and sizes, and so do our thoughts about how to solve them (or maybe avoid them). Stop and think about it. Their lives, just like yours, are collections of everyday decisions. Some are simple. Some are complicated. Some are obvious. Some are obscured. Some are frustrating. Some are satisfying. And no two are exactly alike.

WHY WE DO WHAT WE DO

Conventional wisdom says that people do everything for one of two reasons. They either want to gain pleasure or avoid pain. This means you have two types of decisions:

Gaining pleasure decisions – With gaining pleasure

decisions, you act in hope of making yourself feel better. These are things like learning something new to get a better job, speaking to a stranger to gain a friend, or buying spray-on tanning solution to look good at the beach.

Avoiding pain decisions – With avoiding pain decisions, you act in hopes of avoiding something painful. Driving within the speed limit, buying insurance, and turning assignments in on time are all examples of avoiding pain decisions.

Make a list of all the decisions you made yesterday. Think about whether each one was for gaining pleasure or avoiding pain. Chances are, you'll find that most fit into one category or another. (A few can go either way depending on your self-perception. These include dieting, what you wore, and what you said to that hot stranger in the elevator.)

DECISIONS ARE GETTING HARDER

On top of everything else, many decisions seem to be getting harder. I'm not just talking about the big ones. I'm talking about coffee. Ever stand behind someone who's ordering an extra tall, super hot, double shot, medium twist, espresso in a pre-warmed mug, with low-fat whipped cream, shaken and not stirred? Not only have they wasted ten seconds of their life, they've wasted ten seconds of yours. Have you wanted to yell, "It just coffee!"

There is too much information and too many

choices. There's not enough time and too many details. There's the pressure to do more with less while spending less to get more. There's the time it takes to learn all the new time-saving software so that you can save . . . time.

Walk into a supermarket and try to figure out all the pricing, packaging, labels, and warnings on the 27 types of yogurt you can purchase. Visit a smartphone retailer and ask them to explain the 76 contractual options. Search for shoes online and discover the 432 different styles available. (Okay, I exaggerated. There are only 431.) There are times when we feel like we're spending more time making decisions than enjoying the benefits of what we chose.

HAS ANYONE EVER TAUGHT *YOU* HOW TO MAKE DECISIONS?

At one point or another, someone has said to you, "Just *figure it out*!" First you may have thought, "Yeah, I should." The truth is most people have never been taught a process for solving problems. Since the beginning of time, people learned through trial and error. Try something. Make a mistake. Try something else. Get a little closer. Try once again and so on until you succeed. Then you get that little rush of confidence and think, "Yeah! I did it." Do this enough and you begin to feel like you are successful.

This book is about making decisions . . . not the big strategic decisions that seem to bedevil large organizations and CEOs. This is a book about making the everyday decisions. If you're not good at making them, they can be "sand in the gears" of getting things done.

Let's face it: organizations are nothing more than big collections of decisions. This is true whether you work for the Fortune 500™ or manage the family finances. Some decisions are financial. Some are personal. Some require planning. Some can be made on impulse. In all cases, you live with the consequences. Most are positive. Some are not so positive. A few are negative. And a tiny number are really bad. (Why is it that we seem to remember these in such vivid detail?)

Each chapter of this book is short and most contain a short series of questions at the end. (What better time to work on your decision making than while reading a book on decision making?) What's more, you'll find a 300 word, "chapter before the chapter" which summarizes the essential points.

Finally, you'll find a QR code at the beginning of every chapter. Use this simple technology to access video instruction and other insights about each concept. (Check page ix for information about QR codes and how to use them.)

Figure It Out! This little three-word phase is the key to making smart decisions. But it's not a tool. It's not a strategy. It's not a secret. It's a mindset. Ask anyone who makes consistently smart decisions. They will tell you it is a combination of the habits we discuss in this book. Now let's begin by looking at the three components within *Figure It Out!* and how they can be applied to everyday decisions.

REMEMBER to watch the video connected to this chapter by scanning the QR on the first page.

Decisions can attack you or you can attack decisions. Thinking tactically about everyday problems saves time and treasure.

One

Making Everyday Decisions in Today's Wacky World

Decisions form the foundation of life. The better you get at making them, the more you will thrive. When you make decisions, you live with the consequences. So why not take time to prepare, rather than acting with haste, impatience, and emotion?

Many decisions can be made without too much consideration. But others require considerable thought. It seems like the more important the decision, the harder it is to make. The trouble is most of us have never been taught a formula for problem solving, other than those in math and science classes.

Figure It Out! revolves around the three components

essential to making smart decisions. First, you need to understand the big picture. In other words, the context of
your environment, your particular situation and a host of
other influences will have an impact on the outcome. Second, you need a framework for making the decision. In
this book, I introduce the 5Cs to problem solving – Clarify the problem. Collect your resources. Consider your options. Choose the best option. Cogitate on the outcome.
More about these beginning with Chapter Nine. Third,
you need to perform a "self-instill." In other words, you
need to emulate the behaviors of those who make smart
decisions all the time. There are certain things they do to
ensure success. I identify those in Chapter Sixteen.

If you have the time, check out the story of how I
dealt with a critical, immediate, and expensive decision
using this framework. It begins on page 14.

*   *   *

Why **Figure It Out!**? Because that's what we do all
day, every day. Making decisions is the foundation of
life. The better you get at handling them, the more you
will thrive on the job, at home, in relationships and
everywhere else. (No, I'm not going suggest that you
create a spreadsheet to decide which mate to marry, although this may work for accountants and engineers!)

If you're going to have a family, if you're going to
have a job, if you're going to have a life, you're going

to have problems. Problems require decisions and living with the consequences. So why not get out in front of as many problems as you can by taking a tactical approach?

Figure It Out! revolves around three components. First you have to understand the *big picture*. Whether you're working a job, coaching little league, earning a college degree, or anything else, you have to understand how your effort fits into the big picture. After all, why spend your time on something if you don't know what you get out of it? (More about this in chapter five.)

Second, you need an approach to solving everyday problems. In this book I introduce a five-step process I call the Five Cs:

1. Clarify the problem

2. Collect your resources

3. Consider your options

4. Choose the best option

5. Cogitate on the outcome (Cogitate means to reflect on what you've experienced to define what you've learned.)

The third and final component in becoming a smart decision maker is performing what I call a "self-instill." In other words, you need to emulate the behaviors of those who make smart decisions all the time. There are certain things they do to ensure success. I'll share those in Chapter Sixteen.

CATCHING A FLIGHT TO CLEVELAND

Now, let me relate a personal experience of how all this can work. A while back, I presented an all-day workshop to a group in Des Moines, Iowa. At the end of the event, I drove back to the airport to catch a flight to Cleveland, Ohio. I then planned to drive to Erie, Pennsylvania, check into a hotel, and make a lunchtime speech the next day. The scheduled aircraft for this flight was coming from Chicago. But weather was delaying all air traffic. As time wore on, I became increasingly concerned that my options for an alternate flight were running out. Finally, the inbound aircraft landed. At this point, we were informed that the plane required maintenance and would not depart until 10PM if at all." I immediately went into problem solving mode.

Step 1, *clarify the problem*. I had to get from Des Moines to Erie within the next fourteen hours.

Step 2, *collect your resources*. I had an airline ticket. I had priority status, which might gain me some influence getting on a different flight. I had a credit card for situations just like this. There were rental cars available at the airport. Finally, I have lots of experience working the system when it comes to air travel.

Step 3, *consider your options*. Option one was to take my chances on the scheduled flight. Option two was to find an alternate flight. Option three was to rent a car and drive overnight from Des Moines to Erie. Option four was to charter an airplane. Option five was to call my client and tell him I would not be able to make it. Hmmm. . .

Step 4, *choose the best option*. Based on experience, my little voice told me that the scheduled flight was not going to leave that night. There were just too many phone calls and too much whispering among the staff in the gate area. Alternate flights were out since everything available connected though Chicago. Driving was an option. But Des Moines and Erie are 800 miles apart. Driving through the night in the middle of February seemed ill advised. Then there was chartering an airplane. That would be expensive, but the only other alternative would be to miss the engagement, the first in more than 20 years. In the process, I would have to return the speaking fee deposit and disappoint a lot of people. So the choice became academic, I would try to charter a plane.

I walked over to the fixed base operator (private airplane hanger), which thankfully was a short distance from the terminal. I asked the receptionist who would be able to fly me from Des Moines to Erie. After making a couple of phone calls, she gave me the name and number of someone whom she thought could handle the arrangements. I made the call and explained the details. He told me that there was no way a propeller-driven plane would be able to make it in time. It would have to be a jet. Realizing I had little choice, I told him to find someone to do the job.

He called me back about twenty minutes later. "Are you sitting down?" he asked. The charter fee would be almost exactly the same amount I was being paid to make the speech. (Gulp!) Seeing no alternative, I told him to confirm the flight. Early the next morning, he picked me up at a nearby hotel and we drove to an airfield outside of Des Moines. At exactly 7AM, a small Learjet descended from the sky and rolled up to the hanger. I got on board and two hours later I landed in Erie, PA.

Step 5, *cogitate on the outcome*. As I chatted with the two young pilots that morning, I reflected on what had transpired in the previous eight hours. Yes, the cost of the flight to get me there was consuming the entire speaking fee. On the other hand, I had gotten there on time. Yes, I was out the fee. But I avoided making a very bad impression and letting down several hundred people. Besides, I now have a great story to tell about the challenges of getting someplace when you absolutely, positively have to be there overnight.

Let's continue by exploring the impacts of today's society on the way we all make decisions.

REMEMBER to watch the video connected to this chapter by scanning the QR on the first page.

Are decisions getting harder?
Too many distractions.
Too much pressure. Too few
resources. Too little time.
The answer?

Two

Context, Technology, and Time

The number of decisions we make every day has exploded. There's more pressure and less room for mistakes. Even the stakes for little choices seem higher. If you believed the software companies and marketers, it wasn't supposed to be this way.

So why are decisions getting harder? Lots of reasons. For one, we're dealing with a non-stop pace. From the time you get up until the time your head hits the pillow, there always seems to be something you have to do. Add the continuous entertainment, news crawls, and endless pop-up ads, texting, telemarketers, and social media distractions and you have the recipe for havoc.

The three keys to keeping all this in check are context, technology and time. Context allows you to keep decisions in perspective. By looking at all the challenges coming at you through context, you can better decide what's a priority.

Then there's technology. Software developers will tell you that some application some place will solve all your problems. Smart decision makers know better. Software can only provide data and options based on your input. Too much of this can even confuse the situation. Technology is only a tool, not a solution.

Finally, there's time. We all have 24 hours in a day. But those who are consistently good at making smart decisions successfully prioritize the tasks at hand. They see everything in the context of what's on their plates. They delegate what they don't need to do personally. They dismiss what doesn't need to be done at all. They find linkages between activities to save time and energy. How well do you do this? How could you do it better? Check out Chapters Fifteen and Sixteen for more on this.

*   *   *

I have always been amused by the aggressive drivers who bob and weave through traffic to get one car ahead during rush hour. These individuals inevitably end up at the same traffic light a mile or so down the road. I want to smile and wave when I pull up next to them, but they're probably too dense to get it.

In a way, some of us solve problems this same way. We spend a great deal of effort acting out of impatience, rather than taking the long view and recognizing that planning with care reduces stress and makes for smart decisions.

Over the past few years, the number of daily decisions we all make seems to have increased exponentially. There's the pressure to do more with less. There's the impatience to get things done faster. And a lot of the decisions just seem more difficult than they used to be.

So why are decisions getting harder? Oh, let me count the ways! Some of the reasons are obvious. Some are more obscure. In a nutshell, we're all dealing with too many competing factors for our time and attention. Think about your average day. Chances are, you feel overwhelmed from the time you get up until the time your head hits the pillow. On one hand, you think you're getting a lot accomplished. Look at all the items you can check off your list. On the other hand, you realize that you haven't accomplished as much as you thought. Besides, some of the big decisions had to be put off. Again. Sometimes the days seem to blend from one into the next. Sound familiar?

You might be thinking, "Wait a minute. This is

not a book on time management. Where's the fix? Don't tell me I am overwhelmed. Just get to it. I need to make smart decisions *right now*. I don't have *time* to think about them!"

CONSIDERING THE CONTEXT

I can respond with one word – context. Diction-ary.com defines context as, "the set of circumstances or facts that surround a particular event, situation, etc." When you think about making a decision, any decision, your mind floods with thoughts associat-ed with that issue. If you are selecting what clothes to wear to a party, you'll start thinking about what you've worn in the past. If you want to discipline a child, you'll start thinking about what has worked before. If you think about asking a cute co-worker to lunch, your mind will fill with thoughts about the last time you did something similar. You get the picture.

Context is the key to all smart decisions. Con-text gives you the *why* – why you should do some-thing, why you shouldn't, and the relative risks of each decision. If you don't make decisions through a lens of context, you'll be making dumb decisions. Here are a couple of examples:

Suppose you are selecting a new hire from

among several candidates. They all appear equally qualified, at least on paper. They all said the right things during the interviews. At first blush, it looks like you can throw a dart at their resumes and select one. That's without context.

Then you talk with your colleagues. You learn that one candidate seemed rather flippant about whether he really wanted the job. The other two seemed earnest and interested. But you realize that one lives three times as far away as the other. Should that be a deciding factor? So you're left with a dilemma. No matter what you decide, you are taking a calculated risk. Based on your experience, and the experience of those around you, you'll make the decision. With all things being equal, it's *context* that provides the best insights.

Here's another example. Suppose you've decided to remodel your kitchen. You've obtained bids from three reputable contractors. All have great references, fancy brochures and estimates that are reasonably close. But you've hired contractors in the past. You've learned to ask very specific questions about scheduling and materials. This is where two of the three become evasive about completion. The third is willing to commit to a definite schedule. Once again, the *context* you have, based on experience, allows you to avoid a potentially ugly and expensive situation.

THE INFLUENCES OF TECHNOLOGY AND TIME

I can provide endless examples concerning context. You can, too. Context plays a role in every one of these. To do this, however, we're negotiating with two other influences, *technology* and *time*. Software developers want to convince you that there's an app for everything. But that's not true. These apps will only help you find additional data to add to your context. Some will provide suggestions based on the information you input. But none will ever make the decision for you. You have to do that yourself. If these applications provide too much data, it may even confuse you. Besides, no app will have to live with the consequences of a decision.

In 2001, technology writer Marc Prensky coined the terms, "digital immigrants" and "digital natives" in an article he wrote for *The Atlantic* magazine. Digital immigrants, he argued, are those in society who came of age prior to the introduction of today's digital applications and devices. Digital immigrants developed their problem-solving and reasoning skills *prior* to the menu-driven technology we use today. Since the advent of this technology, they've spent a good deal of time and effort learning how to navigate all this software because their brains are "wired" to approach tasks and problems through a process of trial and error based on experience. Many expect computers to reason, but they don't, do they? I, for instance, can only imagine the number of hours I've spent figuring out all the "easy-to-use" features on my smart phone and laptop. Even with "in-house" tech support (my kids), the world still stops occasionally because I can't open, unlock, navigate, install or upgrade one of these "helpful" gadgets.

Digital natives, Prensky said, are those who have been coming of age immersed in today's environment of electronic cues. They have come to expect that pretty much every decision will be presented in the form of *options*. They are very comfortable navigating through the countless screens on smart phones, tablets, laptops and other devices. They face challenges, however, when there's no right or wrong answer, and no pre-programmed alternatives from which to choose. It's one thing to provide on-line customer assistance where the options are on the screen in front of you, for instance. It's quite another to deal with the unhappy customer across the counter in a store. Decisions like this can be rather than unnerving. The temptation is to reach out for someone else's help whenever this happens. But that's not realistic. Eventually, you have to think for yourself and take a risk that you are making the right decision.

So are you a digital *immigrant* or a digital *native*?

Chances are, you probably feel like you're some of both. That said, you can certainly understand how everyone struggles at times with decisions based on their relationship with digital technology.

The second influence we're negotiating is *time*. We're all given the same amount. But we all seem to be doing more work with fewer resources. Making decisions without taking time to consider context can lead to mistakes. Some people want to "sleep on it." Others want to "think it through." Still others want to put it in their "slow cooker." Whatever your choice of idiom, you have to take time to reflect. Yet many people sacrifice the consideration of context in the interests of getting something, anything, done and out of the way.

Since we all have the same amount of time, the question becomes why some are more effective than others. The answer is simple. They are better decision makers. Smart decisions allow you to leverage your time. This might be through delegation, organization, use of software or some other method. Look around and chances are the people you see having the most impact with their time are also the people who seem to make consistently effective decisions. There's more about this in Chapters 15 and 16.

So how do we deal with this "dumbed-down" world? That's what next.

QUESTIONS TO CONSIDER

- Do your daily decisions seem to be getting harder? Are there more of them? How have you been adapting to this?
- We all have the same amount of time. Do you see some people using it better than you? What can you learn from them?

REMEMBER to watch the video connected to this chapter by scanning the QR on the first page.

We're living in a dumbed-down world. Smart decision makers learn to tune out the noise and distractions.

Three

Making Decisions in Our Dumbed-Down World

Do we really live in a "dumbed-down world?" There's lots of evidence of it. To begin with, there is the technology that wants to help us make every choice. Type some letters into a search engine and up pop lots of irrelevant and distracting suggestions. "I'm searching for tires. But hey, maybe I should check out Tiramisu first." Is that helpful or manipulative? Probably both.

It's also important to consider the media. Today's complicated stories are condensed into 90 seconds or 300 words. Television news seems to move from sound bite to sound bite without time to discuss the impact.

29

No wonder people have tuned out politics, world affairs, economics, and other issues that affect us all every day.

Then there's education. The focus in today's curriculums has shifted to skills and content, without time for process. Applying what you've learned ensures the development of critical thinking skills. Passing a test only demonstrates than you know something, but not if you know how to use it in the real world.

The evolution of public policy has impacted us as well. Policy makers, by nature, have a penchant for control. They also want to protect us from ourselves. The result of this has been an explosion of rules and regulations, many of which have unintended consequences. Zero-tolerance policies are a good example of this.

Then there are the blessings and curses of choices. Endless options seem to appear for every decision. So people are spending more time sorting through unnecessary selections. Some of these are legitimate. But many are simply for the purpose of up-selling the customer or some other manipulation.

Finally we get to the explosion of hyperbole in marketing, media, entertainment, and communication. Making smart decisions is about ignoring the hyperbole and confining your considerations to facts and context.

*   *   *

Now that we've got context, technology, and time out of the way, let's talk about our "dumbed-down world." I am taking a sizeable shot at society when I say the world is dumbing itself down, but someone has to. When we expect all decisions to be easy and convenient, our brains will adapt to this. But when more challenging decisions arise, we will struggle to think in ways that are precise and prudent. For those who are coming of age immersed in this dumbed-down world, the impact is even more crucial.

We see clear evidence of this phenomenon every day. There is "eye-tracking" software being developed to save you the unbearable task of moving a mouse. There is the hotel in New York that offers "work-down calls," to assist you in knowing when it's time to turn off the laptop and go to sleep. Then there are the diapers that text you when the baby needs to be changed. Wouldn't that be obvious? I think the whole idea stinks! (Sorry.)

Outside of technology, evidence of this dumbing down abounds as well. We can begin with the news media. Complicated stories are condensed into 90 seconds or 300 words. Complex situations are reduced to sound bites. Is it any wonder that so many people struggle to understand the political and social issues around them? "Vote for me. I give the best sound bites."

From the media, we can move on to education. Teachers will tell you that today's classes demand exacting instructions and illustrations for all assignments. Students used to ask, "What's on the exam?" and the instructor would answer, "everything." Now students complain if points are deducted for items not specifically identified on the syllabus. Is it any wonder that employers complain about employees who can't seem to think for themselves? (Lest you think I am picking on young people, the average age of today's undergraduate college student is 29.)

Our dumbing down would not be complete without dieting and exercise. "Take this pill and watch your body mass index drop through the floor." "Buy our DVD and have buns of steel and six-pack abs in 21 days." "Click here now and you'll feel pounds lighter immediately" (because someone has stolen the contents of your wallet).

You can even combine all three of these issues by publishing a 200 word article on the wonders of a 21-day dieting class in which there is no homework and no effort, but an automatic "A" for having pecs of perfection. Plus we'll throw in a flawless tan for only three easy payments of $9.99.

THE IMPACT OF PUBLIC POLICY

Much of this dumbing-down is the result of good intentions. We want to simplify. We want to make thinking easier to understand. We want to make things more clear-cut.

Legislation and regulation are good examples. Politicians make countless efforts to protect us from ourselves. But they pass laws without considering the unintended consequences. The vast majority of laws make sense in theory. Implementing each one, however, requires context and depends upon human nature. As the old saying goes, "Rules are made to be broken."

The result of all this good intent has been an enormous growth in rules. But every new rule limits society's ability to reason. Have you ever said to yourself, "That makes no sense," when dealing with a government employee? I certainly have. I've even heard a few of *them* say, "I *know*, I *know*. It doesn't make sense to *me* either."

Over time, all these rules begin to undermine a society's ability to govern itself. This argument may be a little too broad for this book. But think about your workplace. Too many times, rules get in the way of smart decision-making. We are faced with all kinds of conflicting policies and practices. Have you ever come across two rules that contradict each other? Once again, they were well intentioned, but not well conceived.

All of this is made worse by the threat of regulations such as zero-tolerance policies. Have you ever heard someone say, "Never say never?" This three-word phrase is the poster-child for why zero-tolerance policies don't work. Can zero *anything* really work all of the time? Nothing is absolute. When we try to make it so, exceptions come out of the woodwork. Sadly, some in charge attempt to use this type of policy to dodge responsibility. Yes, for example, the first grader carried a butter knife to school in his lunch box. No, the school board should not have expelled him due to the zero-tolerance policy, saying their hands were tied. Yes, someone discovered video of a top-performing salesperson dancing topless as a freshman ten years ago. No, she should *not* have been fired for reflecting poorly on her employer's reputation. If this were the case, firms would be terminating people by the boatload.

THE BLESSING AND CURSE OF CHOICES

Another threat to smart decision making is *choice*, as in too many. Yes, too *many* choices! Now you would think that having more choices would be a good thing. Choices make you feel free. Choices make you feel happy. Choices give you the opportunity to make smart decisions.

Most people associate the number of choices they

have with power. If you can purchase anything you want, people think you have lots of power. If your purchases are limited by financial resources, people think you have less power. Of course, some people make dumb decisions even though they have lots of resources. But I digress.

Even with small decisions, we are being offered too many choices. How many variations of dental floss, pickles, cat food, or canned tomatoes do we really need? The sizes, weights, prices, discounts, nutritional values, and package designs number in the thousands just for breakfast cereal. Some of us are more selective than others, but how much time should we spend deciding what vegetables we want on a Subway™ sandwich?

Having too many choices can result in inertia. Have you ever gone shopping for something, only to be confronted by so many choices that you didn't know where to begin? Perhaps you became frustrated and stopped looking after a while because it felt like too much work to decide. That's what I mean by too many choices causing inertia. You just get stuck.

On the other hand, having reasonable choices taken away by a system that "knows better" can also present challenges. A few years ago, I hosted a meeting at a local hotel. The temperature in the conference room was freezing. I went to the front desk and asked them to turn the heat up a little. The clerk said she didn't know how, but she would check with maintenance. About ten minutes later, one of the hotel managers arrived in the room.

"I'm sorry," he said, "but our heating and air conditioning are controlled by the corporate offices in Atlanta. They have calculated the optimum temperatures to conserve energy and provide comfort at the same time." In disbelief, I asked him, "How do you feel about this?" He forced a smile and said, "I trust you'll understand." Those attending the gathering put on their coats and added, "Move the monthly meeting" to our agenda.

MAKING A LOT OUT OF A LITTLE

This brings us to hyperbole. Dictionary.com defines hyperbole as, "obvious and intentional exaggeration." At the risk of using hyperbole, the hyperbole has gotten totally out of hand. We were all sick of the empty claims made during the last presidential election. Many of us ended up voting for the lesser of two evils. (If you're reading this book 20 years after it was published, chances are nothing has changed.) All this polarizing and demonizing impaired voters' ability to distinguish between candidates and issues. Sadly this is nothing new. It just seems to becoming more intense.

Think of the advertisements that compete endlessly over whose vacuum sucks the best. How about the conflicting health messages about whether it is okay to consume coffee, wine, soda and even tap water. (Why are there expiration dates on bottles of *water*?) And who really thinks all those laundry detergents make your clothes "super bright?"

Making smart decisions is about ignoring the hyperbole. It's about confining your considerations to facts and context. It's about focusing on what's important. Those who make smart decisions act in reasonable ways. Of course this is becoming more difficult with the seeming war on reason in today's culture. Let's address that next.

QUESTIONS TO CONSIDER

- Do you sometimes feel overwhelmed by the number of choices in making a decision? How can you best deal with this?
- Consider the world around you. What impact do daily distractions have on your decision making? How can you do a better job of coping?

REMEMBER to watch the video connected to this chapter by scanning the QR on the first page.

Are you winning the war on reason? How can we make smart decisions when there are way too many rules?

Four

Decision Making and the War on Reason

Do you make decisions by relying on reason or rules? Probably both. Have you noticed that the rules seem to be taking over the reason in more situations? If you think about it, most of your daily decisions impact others. So what impact does this "war on reason" have on your ability to make smart decisions? You have to consider it through a lens of critical thinking.

Critical thinking is considering the context of an issue, coming up with options, and acting on the best option. People who study such things maintain that there is a difference between critical thinking and problem solving. But in daily application, people use the terms interchangeably. In any case, we need to be able to think critically to make better decisions.

Two of the biggest obstacles to today's decision making are rules and digital technology? Why? Because rules limit our ability to reason and digital technology seeks endlessly to manipulate our actions. For tasks related to efficiency and safety, rules and software applications serve a purpose. But when it comes to thinking through relationships, exceptions to procedures, and the occasional transgression, rules can prohibit the obvious from happening. With digital technology, you can find yourself subtly maneuvered in directions the programmers want you to go.

Smart decisions are most often the result of skills and wisdom developed over time. But when rules and digital manipulation get in the way, we become shallower in our reasoning or never develop it in the first place.

*   *   *

The many distracting and confusing rules we deal with every day seem to be overtaking our ability to reason. Don't believe me? Consider your situation. Have you ever tried to complete a project only to be told that it needed to be vetted by the legal department? Have you ever wanted to yell, "Make a decision!" in the middle of a long meeting? Remember the old saying, "A camel is a horse designed by a committee"? That belief is alive and well in many organizations.

Consider the number of special interests that dominate our news, our legislative chambers, and our answering machines. Some politicians refer to them as the fourth branch of government (executive, legislative, judicial, special interests). Imagine the Bolivian Mosquito Alliance lobbying for endangered species status only to be opposed by the Chilean Gnat Federation because of a difference in federal funding. (I made those causes up. But I wouldn't be surprised to hear from those supporting mosquitos or gnats.)

If you think about it, most of your decisions impact others. Sure, your choice of lunch or what to wear is solely yours. (There are exceptions to this, of course. That anchovy and banana sandwich you had for lunch is one of them. So is the polka-dot skirt with the striped top you wore last week.)

Think about where you work. Chances are you can identify some interesting examples. You might be in charge of scheduling staff, for instance. On one hand, you know your decisions affect everyone. On the other, you have to consider how much they impact each person. What about that single Mom who's a hard worker with a crazy schedule? Should you be more flexible with her? Is that fair? Will others be upset? Where is the balance between individual rights and your responsibility to employ and retain hard workers? Do you have enough information? Will this decision impact your ability to supervise these people? Should you consider that as part of your decision?

CRITICAL THINKING

Critical thinking is considering the context of an issue, coming up with options, and acting on the best option. Those who study such things will tell you that critical thinking differs from problem solving. But in everyday application, many people use the terms interchangeably. (The purists will attack me for saying that, but we're talking practical solutions here, not theory.)

Everyday tasks used to be completed manually. If you needed to find a file, you went to the filing cabinet. If you wanted a book, you went to the bookstore. If you wanted to listen to music, you would turn on the record player, the 8-track, the cassette, or the CD player or iPod™. Today it's different. If you need to find a file, you touch a screen. If you want a book, you touch a screen. If you want to listen to music . . . well, you get the picture.

Functionally, there's nothing wrong with this. For simple or repetitive chores, these electronic assists help us do things more efficiently. Here's the challenge. Tasks that require complex reasoning require . . . complex reasoning. We can't assume that there will always be an application to help. Besides, this dependence limits your creativity and view of the bigger picture.

I have always been a little put off by people who include a line at the end of their mobile e-mails that says, "Please excuse any typos. This was sent from a mobile device." I used to think that they should take more care in what they write before sending. But now with the auto-correct feature found on all smart phones, we may have to correct what this "feature" has made incorrect. No long ago, I sent a text saying that I would be home "5ish." The geniuses who programmed this handy little feature decided that the word I was trying to use was "punish." I had watched myself type "5ish" into the phone. But as I pressed "Send," I watched the "helpful" software change "5ish" to "punish." I ask you, is this helpful? Sending nonsense to a loved one may be okay. Sending nonsense to a customer, potential employer, or someone you're trying to impress is something else. Are we now supposed to accept endless typos in communication from others because smart phone producers know better?

At what point do we begin to surrender our thinking skills to software? Oh! Wait a minute! We're doing that right *now*! Do you really want someone limiting your choices of what to purchase? Do you really want someone else deciding which plumber you should hire? Are you comfortable with a bunch of nerds controlling how you should write a letter? Do you want some software endlessly correcting your work with green, yellow, and red highlights? (Yes, you can turn them off. But you need an app to find out how to turn off the app.)

Stand in the middle of a mall, a school or a workplace. You would think that everyone navigates their way through life with their thumbs. My wife and I now text our kids that dinner is ready. Yes, they are in their bedrooms a few feet away.

Smart decisions are most often the result of skills and wisdom developed over time. As a society, we are delaying this development by providing endless technological assists. The result is a culture that looks to a screen for communicating, learning, working, eating, breathing, and sleeping. Are we not sucking the oxygen out of our desire to think? Don't get me started! Oh, wait a minute, I already am! Menu-driven technology is allowing those who seek it to reach the lowest common denominator in thinking . . . total reliance on external cues. ("I looked it up on the Internet and this is all there was.")

Smart decisions have always required focus, research, creativity and calculated risk. In spite of all this technology, nothing has changed. Decisions requiring complex reasoning still require focus, re-search, creativity and calculated risk. The only difference is that we are misleading people into believing that they can work the system rather than work the work.

SO WHAT ARE THE RESULTS OF ALL THIS?

After reading all this, you may be asking yourself, "SO WHAT?" Well, I'll tell you. If you are going to make smart decisions, you need to overcome the forces conspiring against you. If you think that's a little overly dramatic, look around and consider the evidence. We are becoming a society of menu-driven thinkers. We expect to see an array of choices for every decision. We are impatient for closure because there's always too much to do.

When we don't get what we want on our terms, many of us try to work the system to obtain it. That's the logical thing to do if you are fighting nonsensical bureaucracy. In other cases, however, these shortcuts are cheating, not just cheating others, but cheating yourself.

We all seem to be communicating much more. Add the number of text messages and social media posts to the number of e-mails, phone calls, and letters, and it seems like we are just constantly interacting. Of course, most of this takes the form of interruptions. Experts will tell you it takes five to eighteen minutes to regain your concentration after an interruption. There are constant pings, blips, blinks, and flashes alerting us that someone wants our attention. It's a wonder we get anything done!

Smart decisions require a depth of understanding about the issues being considered. But how can we do that when we are communicating in an increasingly shallow way?

Focusing on efficiency sacrifices the depth of meaning. There can be a lack of understanding over even the simplest issues. It is tempting to edit, shorten, abbreviate, and boil down every message to its essence, even if it is no longer clear to the reader.

The upshot of all this efficiency and simplicity are guarded relationships. People are reluctant to express personal opinions or argue for something they believe. But successful persuasion is the result of well-made arguments based on context and an informed position. You can't have one without the other.

Finally, we come to reasoning skills. It is tempting to assume there will always be options from which to choose. For simple decisions, this has been a great help. But what about outcomes involving complex reasoning?

Making smart decisions in a dumbed-down world is about overcoming the temptation to simply go with the flow. After all, those who have an agenda are guiding most of the flow. That agenda may not be in your best interest. Take time to consider the bigger picture and you'll be rewarded with a positive outcome.

QUESTIONS TO CONSIDER

- How does the "war on reason" have an effect on your everyday decision making?
- What can you do to deal with the rules and procedures that challenge your ability to make sound decisions?
- What impact does the "war on reason" have on your relationship with others? How might you resolve this?

REMEMBER to watch the video connected to this chapter by scanning the QR on the first page.

Do you understand the big picture? People who make smart decisions know how to see the issue in perspective.

Five

Reading the Big Picture

How much do you understand about the "big picture?" Do you understand the business model where you work? Have you figured out how the place makes money? If you volunteer at a local shelter, do you understand how the facility functions? Do you periodically take a step back and examine how you and your energy contribute to the overall success of an organization?

The more you understand about the big picture, the better you will be able to make smart decisions in whatever environment you're in. Here's how those who make smart decisions gain this perspective:

First, they ask. As the old saying goes, the only bad question is the one that's never asked. Grow comfortable asking anyone anything. You'll be surprised at the insights and intelligence that are shared. After all, a good portion of how an organization functions is never written down or published in a manual.

Second, they research. This can be reading. This can be attending meetings. This can be watching videos, and a host of other activities. The more you know, the better you are able to predict behavior, reactions, and most importantly the outcomes of your decisions and others'.

Third, they discuss. Adults learn best when they talk about something rather than listening to a presenter or watching a screen. Getting a grip on the big picture means engaging with those around you to test your insights, understand theirs, and detect trends in the organization that may impact how you make decisions.

Making smart decisions requires the ability to block out distractions and focus on the issue at hand within the context of the big picture. In many cases, there is no right or wrong answer. Those who succeed make a habit of seeking out perspective.

*   *   *

Have you ever wondered how the place makes money? You know, the organization where you work. Maybe you're employed by a non-profit agency. Do you know where the money comes from? Sure, you can simply say taxes or contributions. But how does all that happen?

We get up in the morning. We hustle through the workday. We take care of the kids and daily chores. Then we crash back in bed. Our thoughts are all about the tasks at hand. We have three meetings. We have two projects to complete. Then there are the endless e-mails. On top of this, there's a new software to learn. After work, there's a list of things to do at home. There are lots of time-saving products available these days. You'd think life would be simpler. In fact, it's a lot more complicated.

I make a practice of walking up to random people in the organizations I work with. I ask them to explain the outfit's business model. Sometimes, they fumble through a generic explanation. Most times, I get a blank stare. Don't believe me? Try it yourself.

It's not that these people don't care. Chances are, they haven't thought about it. With the press of things to do these days, who's got the time? Besides, they just work in the "bowels" of the organization. Right? Wrong. The individuals we see at the top of any organization started someplace. Many began by throwing themselves into the work at hand. They figured out how they fit into the overall scheme. They learned how to make smart decisions. Over time, people began to notice and opened doors for them.

Even outside of day-to-day business, we need to

understand how organizations operate. Maybe you volunteer at the local shelter or a place of worship. Perhaps you contribute time to a trade association or charity. Maybe you coach community softball. Each one of these organizations operates within a particular framework. Some operate well, others not so much. Each of these groups has their own structure, processes, and economic model. Yes, even your family functions within an economic model, although that can sometimes look rather dysfunctional.

So how does all this relate to making smart decisions? Simple. Making smart decisions requires context. Context is the big picture. The big picture consists of the factors we just discussed. We can all be consumed by the urgent. But understanding the big picture enables us to save time, save money, position ourselves, contribute to the common good, and all kinds of other neat things.

SO WHAT IS THE BIG PICTURE?

The big picture boils down to a clear understanding of the major elements of a going concern. It's about the money. It's about the people. It's about the processes. It's about the strategy. It's about the customers. Now that I've got you thinking, you can probably list a bunch of others.

Many of these factors are not so obvious. In fact,

many of them are hidden from view. Walk into the nearest supermarket, for instance. Pull a box of cereal off the shelf. To purchase it, you might pay $3.89. But how much does the store owner get to keep? Believe it or not, about one percent, or $.04. In fact, there's a saying in the grocery industry – a penny on a dollar. Every organization has costs for doing business. It doesn't make a difference if it's a for-profit or not-for-profit firm. Survey after survey has found that people assume that corporate bottom lines are many times the actual reality.

For instance, to the individuals stocking shelves in our supermarket, all this talk about costs and profit may not mean much. But let's take it a step further. Explain to them that they shouldn't slice too deep with their box cutters when opening cartons of cereal. If they do, they'll damage the packages inside. Each of those damaged packages will be sold at a discount. That discount will erase any profit the store would have made on that cereal. Multiply this by how many times it happens in a week and we're talking real money. It might even have been enough to give each of them a small raise. That's an example of explaining the big picture.

Consider the organization in which you work. What examples can you think of that illustrate how what you do affects the bottom line? I bet you can name several. You've probably complained about other people who just don't understand how your work fits into the big picture.

So how much do you consider these issues when you're making day-to-day decisions? If you're going to make smart decisions, you have to anticipate the needs of the people around you, and the overall organization.

Maybe you volunteer for a local food bank. Organizations like this provide a wonderful community service. But they're also businesses. Where does the food come from? How does it get there? Who organizes it? Who shelves it? Who promotes the food bank to the community? Who keeps track of who's eligible? Who oversees the building and maintenance? Who pays the bills? Who pays the staff? Whew! And that's just the beginning. How do each of these people make decisions? That's all part of the big picture.

Let's talk finances. Why is it important to understand the economic model of an organization? Because "money makes the world go 'round." You may not think of yourself as being a part of the economic model. After all, the decisions you make and the tasks you complete are such a small part of the big picture. Right? Don't believe that for a second. Money always plays a role in the big picture. If you see the context through the lens of the dollars involved you will make better decisions.

Luis, for example, was a maintenance supervisor for a business park that was home to about forty small firms. It was not his job to manage the property's finances. But he had always been curious about how the owner made money. One time over coffee, he asked the owner to explain the business model. The next time they got together, the owner explained all the factors impacting cash flow and how they impacted his investment in this property.

When they came to maintenance costs, the owner went into detail so that Luis would understand how his choice of replacement parts, cleaning supplies, and other materials had an impact on the bottom line. That got Luis thinking about all the decisions he was making that the owner wasn't even aware of. Over the next six months, he figured out how to reduce the property's annual maintenance costs by about eight percent. This amounted to several thousand dollars. That made him a hero in the owner's eyes. Consider how you might use the same strategy. Don't wait for the boss to ask you. Take the initiative. You've got a front row seat on how to improve profit. Just think about it within the context of the big picture.

HOW DOES THE BIG PICTURE IMPACT YOUR DECISION MAKING?

Smart decision making is based on *reasoning*. Reasoning is based on the experiences of trial and error. Trial and error is based on taking calculated (and not so calculated) risks. The calculated ones are the result of understanding context. Context is . . . the big picture.

Many of our daily decisions are made subconsciously. I'm not just talking about driving home without thinking about it. (You do that sometimes, don't you? That's more the result of habit.) I'm talking about what some people call intuition. It's that urge we feel to act in a particular way without having a concrete reason for doing so.

Some people think of intuition as the little voice in their head. Other people say it's their gut. Still others believe it is the voice of God. Regardless of how you interpret its origin, intuition is based on the experiences we've accumulated over a lifetime of learning.

Harvard psychologists Dorothy Leonard and Walter Swap have spent years studying why some people get to the right solution in an instant where others require considerably more time. In their 2007 book, *Deep Smarts,* they write, "We know we are in the presence of deep smarts when we see an expert quickly size up a complex situation and come to a rapid decision — one that proves to be not just good, but wise." They go on to explain that these individuals trust their own judgment even when many opinions are on the table. The authors argue that this is not about arrogance. It is confidence, given their native intelligence and ability to rapidly sort though possible factors and outcomes.

Making smart decisions in this dumbed-down world requires the ability to block out distractions and focus on the issue at hand. You need to draw from your experience and knowledge and think strategically. You might do this once a day. You might do this ten times a day. But you need to commit to this discipline.

HOW DO YOU MARRY SMART DECISION MAKING TO THE BIG PICTURE?

An excellent question! I'm glad you asked. As you'll discover later in the book, the big picture plays a role in the first step of smart problem solving. Some people thrive in an organization. Some don't. The ones who do examine all problems through a lens of the big picture.

In this impatient world of ours, we all face the urge to "just decide something." If we are stumped for an immediate answer, we're tempted to place it on the back burner. Taking time to examine problems through a big picture lens is inconvenient. Sometimes it reveals issues that we don't want to address. (Is ignorance really bliss?)

Other times, a decision might require us to say something or act in a way that stirs a pot. Do we want to use our political capital? Will it create controversy? Would it be a job- or career-threatening move? The answer to all of these is "perhaps."

Smart decision makers accept that life is full of ambiguous situations. Most decisions work out, some don't. But very few are life-threatening. Looking at problems through a big picture lens enables you to predict actions, attitudes, risks, *and* opportunities. If the world were perfect, all the elements of a decision would come together. You would be able to make the best decision because it was . . . the best decision.

But life can be so frustrating. You don't have all the information. The timing isn't perfect. There are too many competing agendas. People are so darned unpredictable! Understanding the big picture is an essential part of smart decisions.

QUESTIONS TO CONSIDER

- How much do you understand about the "big picture" within your work environment? Or where you volunteer? Or where you go to school?
- In what specific ways would you benefit by understanding more about the "big picture" of these organizations?

- What's one step you can take immediately to get a better handle on the big picture?

REMEMBER to watch the video connected to this chapter by scanning the QR on the first page.

Are you starting from neutral when solving problems? Don't let your biases prevent you from making smart decisions.

Six

Getting to Neutral

Let's face it. We all live lives full of distractions, biases, and mistaken assumptions. In order to make decisions that are reasoned, balanced and accurate, we need to get to neutral. This means you need to exclude influences that may interfere with resolving the everyday problems you face.

When I think of these biases and distractions, the 1960s cartoon Ricochet Rabbit comes to mind. He bounced off the walls with a "ping-ping-ping." We bounce off texts, tweets, e-mails, pop-up ads, and non-stop media, not to mention all the pre-conceived notions we might have about the situation.

Those who make smart decisions are able to set these distractions aside and get to a neutral state. Here's what they do:

Clarify the problem. The clearer the idea you have of what needs to be decided, the easier the decision. Chapter NINE addresses this in detail.

Set aside a specific time to consider the issue. Those who make smart decisions set aside dedicated time to think about issues of significance.

Remove yourself from the "environment". With the advent of mobile technology, the definition of environment has changed. These days, "environment" is not just physical, it is mental. Removing yourself means turning off devices, getting away from public distractions and finding a place where advertisements and other chatter will not compete for your attention.

List the distractions and biases about the problem. Listing them forces you to define them. This promotes focus on the true nature of the problem.

Practice reflective thinking. Smart decision makers work at getting to neutral. They have developed a habit of taking time to clarifying problems in a distraction-free environment.

*   *   *

Perhaps you have seen the 2009 animated Disney movie, *Up*. A running gag throughout the film is the word "squirrel." If you have watched the average dog respond to these creatures, you understand the humor. Of course, canine distractions are not limited to squirrels. The same can be said of humans.

I might be treading on thin ice by comparing dogs to humans. But when it comes to everyday life, we all feel like we're at the mercy of whatever is crossing our attention at the time. We can complain about it all we want. It's up to us, however, to take charge of our environment.

The more we allow others to manipulate our choices through technology, the more limited we become in our thinking. The more we listen to endless messages about easy outcomes, the more we limit our true accomplishments. The more we let polarizing messages invade our beliefs, the more biased our beliefs.

We all want to make decisions that are reasoned, balanced, and accurate. In other words, we want to make smart decisions. That's pretty hard when our minds are filled with conflicting distractions. Yes, you need to be mindful of the context. But you must also work to exclude influences that will cloud your thinking. My good friend and veteran educator, Pam Gordon, calls this process *getting to neutral*.

GETTING TO NEUTRAL

Getting to neutral requires that you mentally step away from all the biases you may have associated with the decision at hand. The problem may be big, small, or somewhere in between. Regardless of the size of the problem, we attach our beliefs and perceptions. Some of these are probably accurate. But other perceptions and assumptions can be way off base. Trying to make a smart decision when your judgment is clouded can be a recipe for mistakes and unpleasant consequences. You have to work at getting to neutral. It does not come naturally. There's more about how to apply this principle a little bit later in the chapter.

Serena was faced with a dilemma. She worked as a manager in an insurance company. She was responsible for overseeing a team of adjusters. She had become very efficient at managing time. But the workload continued to increase. One of her biggest challenges was dealing with adjustors who were resisting change. They were used to working at a particular pace. Now they were being asked to improve their productivity. A few of her long-time people had taken to lecturing her. They made sarcastic comments about how the number of mistakes would rise if they were asked to do more.

Serena recognized that there was always that possibility. She also knew that the new software had made that almost impossible. The real issue, she suspected, was that some adjustors were resentful of software that seemed to dumb-down their jobs. They were proud of the skills and knowledge they had developed over the years. They viewed these applications as a threat to their jobs. With that, of course, went their concerns about job security. "After all," one had said, "if any idiot can appraise the damage, why not just have the *customers* fill out a form?"

The big problem for Serena was time. She had more to do and these people were just wasting her time with negative comments and resistance. She knew enough not to act based on her emotions. But she needed to get to neutral. (More about Serena in a bit.)

SO HOW DO YOU GET TO NEUTRAL?

Ricochet Rabbit and his sidekick Droop-A-Long starred in a series of old-west cartoons produced by Hanna-Barbera in the 1960s. Ricochet Rabbit was known for bouncing off the walls with a "ping-ping-*ping*!" as he pursued the outlaws. Don't ask me why, but Ricochet Rabbit comes to mind when I think about today's struggles with focus. Rather than bouncing off walls, we bounce off texts, tweets, e-mails, pop-up ads, and the nonstop music and entertainment in our environment.

Still, there are people who are able to step outside all these distractions and clearly focus on the problem at hand. I call these people *reflective thinkers*. If you observe them, you'll see that they do several things to achieve this state of neutral:

To begin with, **reflective thinkers clarify the problem.** Without having a clear view of the decision to be made, they run the risk of making a poor decision. They might focus on the wrong elements. We'll spend a good deal of time talking about this in chapter NINE.

They also set aside a specific time to consider the issue. Yes, I know. Who's got the time to think these days? It's not our fault, is it? It's all those other people. Their demands are costing us time. We can't set aside time that we don't have to get to neutral! Does this sound familiar?

Well, we should all "get over" ourselves. The essential part of making smart decisions is thinking smart. Let's face it, those who make smart decisions find ways to set aside time to clear their thoughts of biases and distractions.

"How?" you might ask. The secret revolves around two words – *concentration* and *compartmentalization*. Both of these skills are elusive and becoming lost in the uproar of today's non-stop world. For some people, these skills have never been that well developed in the first place. (Sorry, but we have to be honest here.) We wish there were smart phone apps for both of these. (Wouldn't that be cool!) But the simple key to both is to begin practicing them. That takes us to a third strategy.

Reflective thinkers remove themselves from the

environment. With the advent of our mobile culture, the definition of environment has changed. Most people still work in one place. But with a computer in our pocket or purse, many of us are able to work anywhere. With mobile technology, it has become tougher to remove ourselves from the environment.

These days, the environment is not just physical. It is also mental. In today's world, attention is more important than location. We are constantly surrounded by messages craving our attention. You may enjoy being surrounded by all this stimulation. But this makes it very difficult to focus on one issue for more than a few minutes at a time. There always seems to be something popping up on a screen to disrupt concentration.

That means turning off, tuning out, and dropping into a state of focus. (Sounds like Timothy Leary, doesn't it, if you understand the reference.) Smart decision making requires turning off digital distractions. It means moving to a place where advertisements, televisions, and other chatter will not compete for your attention.

If you're a digital native (aged 30 and younger), you may be thinking, "Facebook, Pinterest, Google+, and the rest are *not* distractions. They are how I communicate. I am a digital native. I *can* answer customer questions, write a term paper, eat

lunch, and text my friends, all at the same time."
Don't kid yourself. The truth is your brain cannot
multitask. I've seen the research. (More about this in
the next chapter.) Besides, your friends will not desert
you if you go off the grid for a few minutes. Honest.

Next, **these reflective thinkers list the distractions and biases about the problem.** Then they
work to eliminate them. This helps them bring into
focus the true nature of the problem and what kind
of decision is required. Think about Serena, the insurance manager. What were her distractions and
biases? First, she had a history with these adjustors.
It is reasonable to assume that she had perceptions
about each of them. She may have been more comfortable learning new software than some of her
long-timers. How could she have found the balance
between understanding their challenges and com-
pelling them to use the software? What about the
political environment? Maybe she didn't think the
software worked all that well. Yet her mandate was
to implement it. Hmmmm.

Outside of these emotions, there were the environmental distractions. She had to deal with
constant interruptions and the continual flow of
"urgent" e-mails. Then there was the music being
piped into the office because the division manager
thought that rock-n-roll "kept everybody's juices
flowing." Been there? Done that? Haven't we all?

Finally, **these reflective thinkers practice.** Practice what? Getting to neutral. It is human nature to feel uncomfortable when trying something new. This certainly applies to public speaking, meeting strangers, and skydiving. But it is also true of how you approach problem solving. Develop the habit of clarifying problems. Eliminate distractions and biases. Remove yourself from the environment. The more skillful you become, the more you will become a smarter decision maker in this dumbed-down world.

SERENA AND GETTING TO NEUTRAL

Let's return to Serena's situation. First, she took a short walk to the local coffee shop and bought a snack. She knew that if she remained in the office, someone would find her. Once she had her snack, she sat outside. That way, she didn't have to listen to the music or watch the screens filled with CNN and CNBC.

Second, she wrote down the decision to be made in the form of a *question*. From experience, she's discovered that this is the best technique for clearing her head about what needs to be decided. This may not work for everyone, but it works for her. In this case, the question was, "What steps can I take to balance my adjustors' concerns about using the software with getting them to embrace its use within the next 30 days?" Once she had defined that question, the answers came easily.

Finally, Serena made a list of all the possible issues that might cloud her judgment. Think of the ones described above. Once she had listed them, she was able to exclude them from her considerations. What helped in doing this were the habits she'd developed from doing it many times before. In fact, she is committed to this routine about once per week. When significant decisions come up, she's learned to withhold consideration until she can do some "coffee shop thinking."

So the question here is, "What is the value of reflective thinking when it comes to decision making?" That's simple. Taking the opportunity to reflect allows you to bring forth ideas and associations that present options for making the best decision. Serena recognizes that this is difficult to do in an environment filled with distractions.

You might be thinking, "Serena should just learn to multitask. How does someone who can only think of one thing at a time, get to be a manager?" But that question misses the point. Besides, no one can really multitask. More about that in the next chapter.

QUESTIONS TO CONSIDER

- How can you see "getting to neutral" playing a positive role in the way you make decisions?
- Consider the behaviors of the reflective thinkers identified in this chapter. What can you do to better emulate these practices?

REMEMBER to watch the video connected to this chapter by scanning the QR on the first page.

You can't multitask. Turn off the TV. Ignore the texts. Forget Facebook. Focus on making smart decisions.

Seven

The Myth of Multitasking

Much has been made of multitasking in today's go-go culture. But research tells us that our brains will not allow us to attend to more than one thing at a time. Yes, you can run the dishwasher and dryer at the same time while vacuuming. But that's not the same as texting a friend and comprehending what the customer in front of you has to say. Something is going to suffer (not to mention it's rude).

The obstacle is what brain scientists call "working memory," sometimes called "short-term memory."

Think of working memory as a collection of

sticky notes. All kinds of facts, ideas and environmental stimuli are collected in working memory. But a stimulus in working memory only lasts four to five seconds, less if something interrupts it. Then it is either encoded in long-term memory or replaced by other incoming stimuli. Studies indicate that working memory can hold no more than four stimuli at a time. This includes *everything*, the temperature in the room, someone talking in the next room or the sound of passing vehicles. A loud truck can ruin your concentration, can't it.

If you attend to, or rehearse, a thought, it will reach long-term memory. There, it will be retained as data or as a schema. Data are things like the alphabet. Schemas are formed by mentally assembling a number of related characteristics. (Steering a car, for instance.)

The brain brings data and schemas back into working memory (your attention) based on stimuli. You may not have changed a flat in fifteen years, for instance. But when the right rear blew last week, the procedure for doing so flooded back into your working memory.

The plain truth is that multitasking impairs comprehension. When comprehension is impaired, so is decision making. The more we try to multitask, the less purposeful we become. The more likely we are to rely on the options offered rather than thinking creatively.

*   *   *

A lot has been made of multitasking in today's go-go culture. Because of their skill with computers, many people even believe that the emerging generation has some super ability to accomplish several things at once. Engineers have created a dual-processing computer chip. But our brains will not allow us to attend to more than one thing at a time. Yes, you can have the dishwasher and washing machine going while vacuuming. Yes, you can be printing a report while inputting data. Yes, you can even steer with your knees while texting a friend about the eyeliner you're applying. But suppose the washing machine overflows or the printer runs out of ink. All your attention will turn to those problems. And I don't even want to think about your driving habits.

Have you ever tried to focus on reading a long magazine article with the television on, music in your ears and friends texting you about something or other? Welcome to the world of many teenagers. Is it any wonder, then, that educators say they struggle to get students to read more than 300 words at a time? (And please don't argue that when everything is converted to video, we won't have to read anymore.) While many adults lament this phenomenon, most of them face it as well. Just the activities are different.

The obstacle is what brain scientists call *working memory*. Neuroscience established long ago that there are two basic types of memory, 1) long-term and 2) short-term or working memory.

UNDERSTANDING WORKING MEMORY

Think of working memory as a collection of sticky-notes. All kinds of facts, ideas, and other stimuli are collected in the working memory. These include everything from seeing the people and things around you to the breeze that just rustled the trees outside. Your senses collect all kinds of stimuli and the brain processes those that capture your attention in working memory.

However, through a number of experiments, scientists have concluded that a thought in a person's working memory will only remain there four to five seconds; less if it is interrupted by something. Neuro-research also indicates that working memory can hold no more than three, maybe four, stimuli at the same time. And when I say stimuli, I mean everything. (Scientists call this *cognitive load*.)

Suppose you're working on a project in an unbearably cold room. In addition, other people in the room are yelling back and forth to each other. Are you going to be able to concentrate on the project itself, especially if it's complicated? Chances are, no. Part of your working memory is focusing on the room's temperature. Part of it is attending to what the yelling people are saying. Part of it is focusing on the project. But since working memory can only deal with three stimuli at a time, your ability to concentrate on the project is impaired.

So when you leave that room, you may remember more about how cold the room was than what you actually did on the project. This is because you kept thinking about, or rehearsing, how uncomfortable you felt.

Only a rehearsed thought is transferred from working memory to long-term memory. In other words, you have to think about it for more than four or five seconds. In the process, it is retained, even when new stimuli attempt to replace it. Have you ever had a phenomenal idea in the shower? Have you been unable to remember what the heck it was while you're toweling dry? If you did not rehearse it, this thought was not transferred into long-term memory. (Knowing about this phenomenon, I once jumped out of the shower and wrote the first 100 words of an article I had been assigned. I still have that water-stained sheet of paper.) That brings us to long-term memory.

UNDERSTANDING LONG-TERM MEMORY

Think of long-term memory as a huge filing cabinet. It retains two types of information, *data* and *concepts*. Data can be everything from knowing the alphabet to remembering someone's name. If you can record information in some way and pass it to someone else so they understand it exactly the same way, it's data. Concepts are ideas formed by mentally assembling a number of related characteristics. (What?! Think of ideas such as how to steer a car or how to fry an egg. Obviously, many are a lot more complicated, especially if you add more variables or details.)

Brain scientists call these concepts *schemas*. Schemas are developed as the brain processes what data make it into long-term memory. Imagine taking a course on a favorite topic. As you read, watch, and listen to more and more information about this subject, your brain looks for patterns and connections between all this data. Obviously, the brain is responsible for those "Ah Ha's" that everyone has periodically. This is simply the brain assembling information into a schema.

Interestingly, some scientists believe that the brain does most of its filing and organizing work while you sleep. When the constant stream of stimuli diminishes at night, the brain can use its energy to process the information received the previous day.

During waking hours, the brain brings facts and schemas back into working memory (your attention) based on stimuli. Someone may ask a question in a meeting using a particular phrase. Your brain will bring back into your working memory a daisy chain of thoughts associated with that phrase. You may not have needed to change a tire for fifteen years. But when the right rear blew last month, the procedure for doing so flooded back into your working memory.

You may not have thought about a long lost love since your twenties. Then a similar looking person brushed past you at the Mall. You remembered not only the details of the relationship, you experienced a bit of the emotions you felt when the breakup took place. As individual schemas are brought back into working memory, they are modified by the new information and stimuli present. Then they are re-stored in long-term memory for the future.

I have been teaching people for more than 30 years. I feel most rewarded when someone approaches me at the end of a session and begins their comments with, "*Now* I understand why . . ." It tells me that what I shared has been rehearsed in their working memory. It has also been connected with previous schema. Finally, it has been embedded in their long-term memory for use at a later time. How cool is that?

WHY "MULTITASKING" IMPAIRS DECISION MAKING

Now go back to my example of teenagers, homework, music, and texting and you understand why their attention spans appear lacking. (There's a lot more to this, but you get the point.) When the brain is overwhelmed with too many competing and continual stimuli, it simply shuts down, just like a frozen computer. You may not have to press Control-Alt-Delete, but the effect is the same. This is the reason, for example, why reading comprehension drops like a rock when students listen to music, update Facebook, or catch up on *Survivor* while doing their homework. Of course this is not just about distracted students, is it? Simply put, those who think they can multi-task are fooling themselves.

The more we try to multitask, the less purposeful we become. When we aren't purposeful, we are less able to reason through a problem. We are more likely to rely on conventional ideas instead of thinking more creatively. In other words, we become reliant on the options and choices offered us by others.

About this phenomenon, playwright Richard Foreman has written, "We risk turning into pancake people – spread wide and thin as we connect with that vast network of information accessed by the mere touch of a button."

The speed and complexity of the world continues to increase. We will continue to deal with more and more distractions that promise convenience, ease, and perfect outcomes. Our ability to navigate the competition for our attention will become more and more intense. We have to develop a strong set of habits around concentration and compartmentalization. These habits will thrust you in front of those who succumb to the closest screen.

But smart decision making is about more than just understanding why our world seems to be conspiring against our efforts to do so. It's also about learning and using a framework for problem solving upon which we can rely when the answer isn't obvious, nor offered on a screen. That's what we'll cover in the next section of this book.

QUESTIONS TO CONSIDER

- Consider your work and home environments. How much of a multitasker are you? How well does it work?
- After reading this chapter, what can you do to better manage the pressures to multitask?

REMEMBER to watch the video connected to this chapter by scanning the QR on the first page.

How do you solve problems? Try the 5Cs – Clarify, Collect, Consider, Choose, Cogitate.

Eight

An Introduction to the 5Cs

A wide range of books have been written about critical thinking, problem solving, and decision making. Many contain some great insights. The trouble is they're all too long and involved to help you with the everyday problems. What you need is a simple framework that can be applied to every situation.

The truth is, no one ever teaches us how to solve problems in a tactical way. Sure, if you're the CEO, someone has taught you strategic planning and mentored you through the BIG decisions. But chances are, you're in the trenches trying to make a positive contribution and thrive within the environment. Those types of decisions require down-to-earth thinking. That's what the 5Cs framework is all about.

Different generations approach decisions using different methods. Older generations grew up solving problems using trial and error. In spite of today's technology, most of them still begin with that approach. Those coming of age with digital applications turn first to screens for answers. Over time these are melding together. But there is still nothing that replaces judgment based on experience and intuition.

No one grows without discomfort. That's the bottom line. But applying a simple framework to whatever challenges you face will force you to take a momentary step back and think strategically. That's what we cover in the next five chapters.

*   *   *

A colleague of mine tells of receiving a call from her son who was a freshman at college. The fact that he called rather than texting told her it must be serious. "Mom," he said, "I am in the laundry room and I'm scared."

"What's *wrong*?" she asked

He went on to explain that he'd always ignored her lessons on doing laundry when he lived at home. But now that he was on his own, the proper use of washing machines had become an essential skill. The last thing he wanted was pink and purple underwear. After providing a few patient instructions, she could tell he was relieved and determined to master this vital task. It's funny how everyday problems can take on crisis proportions when you're faced with "do or dye" decision. (Sorry.)

Search on-line and you'll find lots of approaches to critical thinking and problem solving. Some are rather straightforward. Others are complicated and hard to follow. I know. I've reviewed lots of them. All this research can be helpful to those interested. But it is close to impossible to use these theories for solving everyday problems. How do you deal with that angry customer? How do you resolve the college registration issue? What do you do when the car breaks down? How do you resolve that issue with a co-worker? No one has time to apply some complicated formula when that angry customer is standing in front of you.

What you need is a simple framework that can be applied to every situation. But think for a moment. Has anyone outside of math class ever sat you down and said, "Here's how you solve problems?" Probably not. Most people learn how to solve problems by stumbling their way to solutions. This usually happens after a number of mistakes and mishaps. Over time, they learn from these mistakes and become wiser about what to do. If you use this trial-and-error approach

enough, you become pretty good at figuring things out.
All this takes time, of course. In this impatient world,
there's not a lot of that to go around.

IMMIGRANTS, NATIVES AND PROBLEM SOLVING

The digital immigrants I referred to a few chapters ago
have had an advantage in this area. Yes, an advantage! You
see, prior to today's menu-driven software, they learned to
solve problems the old-fashioned way. They made lots of
mistakes. They also learned to solve problems much earlier
in life. Why? Because their parents and others would tell
them to "figure it out." That might sound cruel and un-
parent-like in today's world. But this approach taught digital immigrants to be creative and resourceful when faced
with daily challenges. Don't believe me? Ask a few of them.
Chances are they'll confirm this experience.

If you're a digital native, you've had a different journey. You've grown up immersed in a menu-
driven culture. You have learned to navigate your
way through most of every day using the screens in
front of you. Want to connect with friends? *Facebook* them. Searching for a new car? Go to *cars.com*.
Need research for a term paper? *Google* it. Looking
for a local restaurant? Whip out the smart phone.

But what about life outside the screen? How
about that co-worker who bugs you? You can't just

"unfriend" him. What about that angry customer? You can't go to angrycustomer.com and review your options. What if your car breaks down? No website is going to get the mechanic there faster. Then there are those situations at work, at school or at home where you just have to use your judgment and live with the consequences.

HAVE YOU EVER GROWN WITHOUT DISCOMFORT?

I may ruffle a few feathers here. But I firmly believe that all the theories in the world are not going to improve your problem solving skills. You just have to step out into the unknown when these challenges arise and use your smarts. Will you be uncomfortable at times? Yes. But as a close friend has asked me more than once, "Have you ever grown without discomfort?" (I have to be reminded of this regularly myself.)

Several years ago, for example, I chaperoned one of my daughter's middle school field trips. The purpose was to explore the role of government in society. We began by walking a half-mile from the school to the nearest bus stop and taking the #7 into the city. Learning about government was one part of the day's agenda. Learning to navigate the city and its public transportation was the other. The teachers made it clear that chaperones were there to support, not instruct. They wanted the kids thinking on their own.

Once downtown, the class spent the day in groups of four or five, proceeding from one assignment to the next. We visited the state capitol and sat in on a session of the legislature. We visited the election commission to find out how to run for office. We sat in traffic court. We went to city hall and asked what it took to reserve a picnic area in a local park. We visited the child welfare office.

Finally, the students had to approach five people on the street and ask them what role they thought government was playing in their lives. That exercise, in itself, was informative, entertaining, and, in a few cases, disappointing. As an adult, I learned things about government that I didn't know. I was also shocked about how little most people the kids interviewed understood about government's role in their lives.

As much as there was some initial discomfort about meeting strangers and asking for information, they all survived and even thrived. Part of making smart decisions is getting past the uneasiness of the unknown. When you get that experience under your belt in middle school, you come out ahead of the game later on.

Applying a simple framework to whatever challenges you face will force you to take a momentary step back and think strategically. Over the next five chapters, you will learn a simple process for solving any problem, regardless of the time allotted. I call it the 5 Cs to problem solving. (This does not apply to calculus and the other hard sciences, of course. They're a whole different animal.) So, let's begin.

QUESTIONS TO CONSIDER

- Do you consider yourself a digital immigrant or a digital native? Why?
- Consider the last time it took some discomfort to "grow" through a significant decision. What did you learn?
- What did you take away from this experience that made you a smarter decision maker?

REMEMBER to watch the video connected to this chapter by scanning the QR on the first page.

If you haven't clarified the problem, the decision becomes that much harder. Take time to think before acting.

Nine

Clarify the Problem

When was the last time you thought you understood the problem only to find out you were wrong? Outside of the digital environment, most significant decisions are more complicated than they initially appear. On a computer, you are offered options. In the rest of life, you're pretty much on your own.

Clarifying the problem anchors the rest of the decision making process. Besides, this is the key to saving time, reducing stress, and feeling good about your ability to navigate in today's overwhelming world. So what are the keys to clarifying a problem? Ask five simple questions:

1. What does success look like? When the problem has been resolved, how will you know? Will there be agreement? Will there be a completed project? How will you describe the resolution?

2. Who are the stakeholders? Who will be affected by this decision? Are there hidden or silent stakeholders you should be aware of?

3. What's the timing? Does this problem require immediate resolution? Compared to other priorities, where does it fall? Who's priority is this? Are you in a position to influence the timing if necessary?

4. What is the gravity of this problem? How important is this problem in the "big picture?" Should you be making the decision? Can you delegate the decision to someone else? Should you?

5. What is your level of investment? How much energy do you want to contribute to this decision? Will the effort be worth the outcome? Are you getting sucked into someone else's mess?

Whatever the problem, take time to clarify what needs to be accomplished. Don't dive headfirst into a decision without answering all the questions above.

* * *

Have you ever tried to solve a problem only to discover that the situation was more complicated than you thought? Perhaps what you assumed to be fact turned out to be someone else's opinion? Perhaps the assumptions you made based on past experience were blown out of the water by new information. Maybe a new boss was added to the equation and he upended everyone's approach to the work.

Outside of the digital environment, many problems are like this. On a computer, you are offered options. Click on an option and you know what you're going to get (unless you're using a search engine). Making decisions while using a computer, smart phone, tablet, or other device is, for the most part, predictable.

In the rest of life, you're pretty much on your own. You can ask for help. You can gather ideas on the web. You can thrash about thinking of options. But regardless of what you do, the decision belongs to you. What's more, you can't press *escape* or *undo* if you guess wrong.

You might be trying to overcome a misunderstanding or resolve a customer's frustration. Problems based on relationships can be particularly complex. You may have been assigned a task, only to discover that you been given incomplete directions. Maybe your cat has gotten away and you have no idea where to begin the search. If I gave you a few minutes, you could probably fill a page with all the similar problems you've faced.

Did you take a step back, however, in each one of these situations and determine the actual problem needing to be solved? Probably not. But this is the key to saving time, reducing stress and feeling good about your ability to navigate in today's overwhelming world.

Take a look at the situations above. If you're trying to resolve a customer's issue, have you really clarified her concern? Have you stated the problem back to her as you understand it to make sure you've got it right? You might say something like, "So you weren't happy with the quality of the product. Is that correct?" This offers the customer an opportunity to confirm your perception, or correct it if necessary. Then you can move forward with the right solution, knowing that you're on the right path.

Suppose you haven't been given all the instructions for the task you were assigned. Rather than stewing about what to do, you might return to the person assigning the task. Say something like, "I've looked through what you want me to do and there appears to be a missing step. Would you take a minute to review this with me to make sure I'm on the right track?" Chances are, he or she will discover the mistake.

And then there's your missing pussycat. Before rushing out the door on a search-and-rescue mission, it's a good idea to stop and consider all the places she has hidden in the past. When it comes to pets, we all tend to replace our rational thought with emotions. Stopping to verify what actually needs to be accomplished reduces heartburn and saves time.

All kinds of time-saving technology have been introduced over the past decade. But we still find ourselves feeling more overwhelmed than ever before. Several factors have contributed to this:

1. The time it takes to learn how to use all this time-saving software;

2. The expectation that we can all do more due to this time-saving software;

3. The expectation that we all must do more with less because of tough economic times;

4. All the companies selling time-saving software that make us feel like we're standing still because we're not using their product and;

5. Our own sense of insecurity because everyone
    around us seems to be getting five times more
    done in the average hour than we do. Who can
    compete with those people? Who would want
    to? Working harder and working smarter are
    not the same thing.

But there is a problem with this approach. We don't stop
to clarify how best to approach the challenge. If we don't
stop to think, we risk solving the wrong problem or one
that doesn't exist. (Have you ever done that? I certainly
have!)

THE KEYS TO CLARIFYING EVERYDAY PROBLEMS

So what are the keys to clarifying a problem? Ask
five simple questions:

1) *What does success looks like?* When the problem
has been resolved, how will you know it has? Will there
be agreement between the people involved? Will someone
have accomplished something? Will there be an obvious
outcome? How can you best explain this resolution to
others? Explaining the problem concisely will frame what
needs to be accomplished.

2) *Who are the stakeholders?* Who is affected by this
problem? Sometimes there is a silent or hidden stake-

holder. That person might be the boss' boss. It might be the customer's boss. It might be the assistant principal, rather than your child's teacher. Take a few seconds to look past the obvious players. Who has the real influence on the final decision? Realtors have learned, for instance, that women are the main influencers in purchasing most houses. They've also learned that the main factor influencing women is the design and condition of the kitchen. (This may sound sexist. But when your sales commission could be thousands of dollars, you go with what works.)

3) *What's the timing?* Is this a decision that needs to be made right away? Can it wait? Should it wait? (Sometimes it's best to reflect on something before acting.) Is there an urgency imposed by someone else? Can this person force you to act in haste? Are you imposing this urgency on yourself? Obviously, there are degrees of all this. If the customer is standing in front of you, you may have to decide right away. On the other hand, the urgency of this problem may have been someone else's doing. ("Lack of planning on your part does not constitute a crisis on my part.")

4) *What is the gravity of this problem?* In other words, how important is it in the big picture? We've all found ourselves involved with a decision about something that shouldn't really deserve anyone's attention. Chips or pretzels? Chocolate frosting or vanilla? Over or under? I am referring to toilet paper rolls here. (I will concede that this last issue *can* get contentious.)

At times, there's no avoiding the importance of the decision. This is especially true when the boss has assigned you the task. But that does not mean you have to invest a lot time or attention in the outcome. Whether you choose chips or pretzels, someone will always be unhappy. So just make a decision and move on. If someone is that dismayed with your choice, next time *they* can choose.

5) *What is your level of investment?* Finally, consider how much energy you want to contribute to the problem. How will it affect you? Will the effort be worth the outcome? It is easy to get sucked into someone else's mess. There may be outside forces influencing your level of interest. But many times there's not. So take a second to consider your actions before diving headfirst into making a decision with little return for you.

What about all those people around you who seem to be working non-stop? What about those people who dive in without thinking? What about those people who seem more interested in getting *anything* done more than the *right* thing done? Ignore them. For all you know, they're spinning their wheels.

What about those people, especially bosses, who ask why you're just standing there? How about the friend or co-worker who comments that you seem to be slowing down. Explain that you are thinking through exactly what needs to be done so you don't waste time. Who can argue with that?

Whatever the problem, take time to clarify what needs to be accomplished. It is the essential first step in making smart decisions.

QUESTIONS TO CONSIDER

- Consider a decision you are in the process of making. Answer the five questions on page 96.
- What is the one habit you can develop to better clarify the everyday decisions you face?

REMEMBER to watch the video connected to this chapter by scanning the QR on the first page.

Collect all your resources before trying to solve a problem. Remember, not all of them can be found on a screen.

Ten

Collect Your Resources

It's easy to feel all alone when you're making decisions, especially the big ones. But you are surrounded by resources, if you make a habit of looking. Not all of today's resources come from a screen, of course. Yet some people really think so. In spite of today's technology, the majority of information still comes from other people, through questions and conversations. Sure, you can find facts and data on-line. You can also find other people's opinions and instructions. In some situations, these resources provide the context or insight to make smart decisions. When it comes to pulling the trigger on something significant however, it is best to discuss, argue, and hash over your considerations with friends or colleagues.

Resist the temptation to act out of emotion when the pressure is on. Act with deliberation. Don't worry about appearing foolish or making a mistake. The same people who worry you have their own fears and uncertainties.

Different generations think differently about collecting resources. Digital immigrants are more likely to think back to their experiences or consult long-time friends. Only then will they search on-line. For digital natives, the reverse appears to be true. They will turn to screens first or send a text to their many on-line connections. If this does not yield helpful insights, they will consult resources not found through digital technology. Surveys indicate that young people are more collaborative in their decision making, while older individuals tend toward solitary consideration. There is more and more collaboration taking place, however, as software becomes easier to use and young people see that older generations possess many valuable insights.

Will everyone you ask be able, or willing, to help? No. But it's always best to ask, even if you are uncertain of their response. Once again, have you ever grown without discomfort? The key to collecting your resources is to act with deliberation. Look past the obvious information and dig for the insights and assistance that will appear only if you ask. Those who make smart decisions are thorough in their collection of resources.

*   *   *

It's easy to feel like you're all alone when making decisions. This can be especially true if there is no clear answer. Maybe you don't have a lot of time to resolve the situation. Perhaps you've made a mistake in a similar situation and you don't want to do it again.

If you stop and think, there are lots of resources from which to choose. The world seems to demand immediate answers. Your gut might tell you to guess your way through. But this can lead to all kinds of havoc.

Resist the temptation to act out of emotion. You might think the pressure is on. But is it really? You might fear looking foolish if you do the wrong thing. Let's be honest here. Is anyone really going to notice? They're probably dealing with their own fears and uncertainties. You get the picture. Instead, gather your thoughts and consider where and how you might find the resources you need. If you stop for a minute and look around, there's help all over the place.

Orvel Ray Wilson, a good friend of mine, tells the story of being promoted to sales manager of his employer's location in San Diego, a great opportunity. But then came the kicker. "We're closing this office in Albuquerque," his manager had said. "You need to pack up all these files and equipment and be open for business in San Diego in 36 hours." Orvel Ray's first urge might have been to panic or assume it couldn't be done. Instead, he considered his resources.

The first challenge was to find enough boxes to pack the old office. After driving around to lots of supermarkets and liquor stores, he had found what he needed. (This was prior to the big box stores where you can purchase boxes for a buck.) Then came the challenge of renting a trailer to carry everything. After lots of phone calls, he found one. Then the office and his apartment needed to be packed. Challenge after challenge was overcome by collecting resources and acting on them. Thirty-six hours later, he was managing the new sales office in San Diego. If you look around, you'll discover countless examples like this one, where people rose to the occasion and solved the problem. Chances are, you have overcome a few yourself.

Most of our problems are not that dramatic. They mostly require you to make a simple decision and live with the consequences. We do this every day and don't give it a second thought. Regardless of the challenge, stop to gather the resources you need. It will save time and heartburn. (This is why taking time to clarify the problem beforehand is so essential.)

COLLECTING YOUR RESOURCES

So where do the resources to solve a problem come from? That might sound like a silly question, but it depends on your perspective. Those in their twenties might turn immediately to a laptop, smart phone, or tablet. That's not to say that they don't know they can look elsewhere. It's just become second nature to begin with on-line resources. Do they seek the input of others? Sure, but they are more likely to reach out digitally than to call people together for a face-to-face conversation.

Those in their sixties are more likely to rely on memories, experiences, and long-time connections with others. As I write this in a coffee shop, for instance, I am seated next to a group of elderly men who are swapping stories, some of which get "better" every time they're told. The topics vary widely, but every once in a while they will come around to home or automobile repair. They'll explain to each other their methods for fixing that leaky toilet, repairing drywall, bracing a sagging porch, or some such thing. Add the experience of these individuals together and you have more than 100 years of solutions, based on trial and error. They might argue, "Who needs the Internet? We have each other." But they'd be wrong. On the one hand, those in their twenties can learn something from meeting rather than texting friends. On the other, digital immigrants can learn a bunch from the on-line videos, manuals and articles that are available at the touch of a screen.

Here's an example of this in action. I spoke with a gentleman who owns a number of "rent-all" locations. Each location employs a mechanic who repairs and maintains the equipment being leased. Many of these individuals are longtime technicians who have been working on equipment for years. A few are relatively fresh from training at a local community college.

Occasionally, each of these mechanics will get stumped by a broken machine. Since they all work alone, they have to use their wits to solve these challenges. It has been the nature of the seasoned mechanics to dig back in their memories for solutions. If that doesn't work, they call a couple of friends for ideas. The young mechanics, not having this depth of experience, search the web or send a text to a number of friends. Over the next hour, they generally receive half a dozen or more suggestions, solutions, and links.

As on-line resources have become more a part of our lives, the veteran technicians have begun using their smart phones to search for ideas from around the Internet. In other words, ten million heads are better than one. Of course, sorting the good information from the bad requires a basic level of discernment.

At the same time, those fairly new to the positions are reaching out to their veteran colleagues. Why? Because it's one thing to get a snippet of advice from a text message. It's quite another to implement it, especially if you have never performed the task before.

You might be able to search on-line to find what you need. This works well for gathering instructions and facts. But most of the time it becomes a matter of asking the people around you. After all, decisions with any significant gravity require your judgment. You could be right. You could be wrong. You could make things better. You could make things worse. Why not take time to ask for input from others who might know better? Of course, all this assumes that you know what you're looking for or at least have a basic idea. If not, stop and clarify your problem.

WILL EVERYONE HELP?

Will everyone you ask be able to help? No. Will everyone you ask be willing to help? No. On occasion you might even find a person who can give you the answer, but says, "Figure it out." That may appear to be mean-spirited at first. But chances are, they are doing it because they believe you can solve the problem and need to learn how. As I asked before, have you ever grown without discomfort?

Events and personal experiences shape our view of the world. Different generations respond in different ways to the problems they face. The digital immigrants that I've referenced before might turn first to family, friends, or co-workers for insights and ideas. They might put on their "thinking caps" and draw on past experience. Increasingly, they are also searching the World Wide Web for answers.

In any case, these trial-and-error thinkers are generally comfortable seeking the help of others. (As women have observed, male drivers asking for directions are exceptions to this.)

Digital natives think differently. For many, the first urge is to reach for the closest screen and rev up their thumbs, track-pad, or mouse. Of course, sometimes it is more efficient to ask someone who can give a quick and specific answer. A tremendous amount of information can be found on-line. But collecting most resources is still a matter of consulting with others. Just the methods have evolved over the years. There's nothing like asking for a person's insights. Besides, the goodwill this engenders can be priceless. Asking for directions on a street corner anywhere in the world, for instance, will still elicit a helpful response 99% of the time.

So, is there a specific system for collecting resources? Not really. The key is to be thorough. Some people just number to ten on a page and then brainstorm all the ways they can think of. Others send a text to trusted friends and colleagues asking for suggestions. Some get on the phone and make a few calls. The key is to seek insights from others. You don't want to obsess over collecting every last idea. But you want to know that you've made a concerted effort at collecting the most helpful information available. So now that you've collected your resources, let's talk options.

QUESTIONS TO CONSIDER

- How dependent are you on the Internet to find the resources you need to make decisions? (Be honest.)
- What are the one or two steps you can take to improve your resource-collecting practices?

REMEMBER to watch the video connected to this chapter by scanning the QR on the first page.

Consider all your options when making a decision. Don't let emotions, pressures, and others' agendas cloud your wisdom.

Eleven

Consider Your Options

Another key to making smart decisions is to act with deliberation. In this crazy, busy, and demanding world, your urge might be to just do something. But too many times, that results in careless mistakes or worse.

Problems come in all shapes and sizes. Those who make smart decisions are careful to examine all the reasonable options. To do this, of course, requires stepping away from emotions, yours and others.

Once you've stepped away from emotions, you

can take a step back and look at all the options evenhandedly. Can you handle the decision yourself? Do you need to? What are your alternatives? Would it be better to collaborate with someone else?

Sometimes time is of the essence. But most of the time, it is not. So take every opportunity to consider your options in whatever way works best for you. After all, you're the decision maker. Be receptive to others' input, but remain confident and decisive.

Those who make consistently smart decisions have developed a habit of setting aside time to brainstorm the alternatives they might pursue. There is no rule for identifying options. Some make a list. Others create a bubble diagram. Still others stand in front of a white board and jot ideas. Some talk the situation though with others. A few take a walk and think. You have to do what works *best* for you. But developing a reliable strategy for considering options will produce the inspiration you need.

*   *   *

Have you ever had a decision blow up in your face? Maybe what you did seemed to be obvious. Then you watched it unravel. Have you ever acted in haste? Someone was tapping his foot and giving you that "Make a decision!" look? So you acted and it turned out to be the wrong choice?

We've all been there. One of the keys to making a smart decision is acting deliberately. As the old saying goes, "Haste makes waste." Don't let the pressure get to you.

Instead, take a few moments to consider your options. Think about being face-to-face with an angry customer. Sure, you feel a pressure to act immediately. You can sense that person's impatience. You can see their glare of disgust. Put yourself in that person's position. Would it be reasonable if the salesperson excused herself to seek the right assistance? Chances are, you would think so. You can do the same thing. The customer has no choice but to go along, provided you do it politely.

Once you've stepped away from the emotions of the situation, you can better consider your options. Can you handle this challenge yourself? If so, what are your alternatives? Would it be appropriate to bring a manager into the picture? If so, what specifically would you like him or her to do? Is there a co-worker who would be better suited to resolving this? Why? How would you explain what needs to be accomplished? You can think of ideas like this in the time it took me to type them.

You may not work in retail. But these principles hold true in any situation. Whether you're at work, at home, or in the company of friends or strangers, you always have the opportunity to take time and think about the best way to proceed. You might ask others. You might make a list. You might even ask the person who's waiting for your decision.

Can you really ask the customer, "What would you like to see happen?" Believe it or not, most people are reasonable in their expectations.

Sometimes, time is of the essence. But most times it's not. So take the opportunity to consider your options in whatever way works best for you. Remember, deliberation beats haste and ensures a better outcome.

CONSIDERING OPTIONS

Here's an example. Brian manages a sporting goods store in the Midwest. When the chain decided to run a big sale over a holiday weekend, he realized that his four cash registers would be overwhelmed. Not wanting to lose sales or customers because of long lines, he started searching for a solution. He could bring in a few more cash registers. But most people pay with credit or debit cards these days. Obtaining additional credit card terminals would take too long. He could move the four registers he had around the store to make them more accessible. But that might confuse his regular patrons who were used to the store's layout. He could ask headquarters to delay the sale while he made space for more registers and credit card terminals. But after the sale, he would no longer need the space and equipment. Besides, other stores were figuring it out.

Then he discovered Square.com. Square.com™ allows users to accept credit and debit card payments using a mobile device. Brian proceeded to set up several of these accounts on employee smart phones with the funds collected being directed into the store's local bank account. His increased sales that weekend more than made up for the fact that he didn't ask headquarters' permission before making this decision. Sometimes, you just have to do what you have to do.

Here's another example. For a number of years, I worked as a career counselor. I conducted hundreds of practice interviews with college students who were about to graduate. When it came to marketing majors, I would wait for the right moment and place my fancy pen in front of them. "Sell me that pen," I would say. "You have thirty seconds to prepare." In most cases, the students would say, "That's not fair" or they would stumble their way through some made-up features that they hoped would seal the deal.

In a few cases however, the student would turn the tables on me. "Tell me about how you and your employees use pens," he or she might say. "How many pens will you need? How many pens does the average employee go through in a given year?" Instead of simply diving into a solution, these individuals took the time to think through the challenge. They displayed the confidence to ask for clarification before acting without thinking. In doing so, they were able to explore options that would solve the problem.

Those who make consistently smart decisions have developed a habit of setting aside time to brainstorm the alternatives they might pursue to make the best decision. There is no rule for developing options. Some make a list. Others create a bubble diagram. Still others stand in front of a white board and jot ideas. Some talk the situation though with others. A few simply take a walk and think. You have do what works *best* for you. But developing a reliable strategy for considering options will produce the inspiration you need. So let's lets talk next about choosing the best option.

QUESTIONS TO CONSIDER

• When was the last time you made a significant decision without considering all the options? What was the outcome?

• What's the one step you can take to better consider your options when making significant decisions?

REMEMBER to watch the video connected to this chapter by scanning the QR on the first page.

Choosing the best option is all about calculated risk. Smart decision makers look at all the options, not just the obvious.

Twelve

Choose the Best Option

Acting on any decision can be the hardest part. After all, there's no going back. In many cases, this is no big deal. But in some, the pressure is on. There's no escape key. The undo button doesn't work. Everything's on the record. This is when taking time to deliberate on the resources you've collected and the options you've identified pays off.

There are three variables in every decision – information, importance, and emotion. The keys to useful information are accuracy and relevance. You have to believe that you have good information and that it applies to the problem you're solving. Even when others try to dissuade them, those making smart decisions choose the best option because of these two elements.

Is it possible to make a mistake in spite of careful deliberation? Sure. There might be a factor or two outside of your control, such as a boss who wants his way. But if you are at peace with your decision, mistakes become a teaching moment rather than a disaster.

The next variable is importance. But importance to whom? Answer two questions when making decisions that will have a lasting impact: 1) How important is this decision to me? 2) How important is this decision to the people it will impact? The answers will provide you with valuable perspective on how to act.

The final variable in choosing the best option is emotion. The emotion associated with a decision can be placed on a sliding scale. Left or right in the parking lot? Who cares? Enlisting in the military? That can get you worked up. Your emotions may not be the only ones involved. You *may* need to consider this impact as well. But remember to consider this within the context of the overall decision.

*   *   *

Keeping restaurant patrons comfortable can be a challenge. Someone always seems to be too cold or too warm. The manager of a restaurant I worked in years ago explored a number of possible solutions. He thought about placing a sign close to the front door informing everyone that the restaurant temperature was maintained at a constant 72 degrees. He considered training all his staff on how to diplomatically explain to customers the problem with keeping everyone comfortable. He even thought about running soup specials on hot days for those who were never warm enough.

Then he started thinking outside the box. He installed a thermostat on the wall in a prominent place in the dining room. No one was allowed to touch it except the manager. When someone complained about the temperature, he would walk over to this thermostat and adjust in full view of the customers. Then he would assure the person who was too cold or too hot that things would get better in a few minutes. The thermostat, of course, was not connected to anything. He never received a complaint. Sometimes people will fix their own problems if they know you're paying attention.

THE VARIABLES IN ALL DECISIONS

The three variables in all decisions are *information*, *importance*, and *emotion*. Let's begin with information. We have spent time discussing the value of information already. We've talked about determining the true nature of the problem. That's information. We've talked about collecting resources. That's information. We've talked about considering our options. That's information as well.

The keys to useful information are *accuracy* and *relevance*. In other words, can you believe what you've learned and does it apply to your problem? People who consistently make smart decisions have developed a practice of choosing the best option based on these two criteria. This is true even when others try to dissuade them. Sometimes a friend or colleague will push for a particular option. When this happens, they will assume that some sort of agenda is involved. This is when they become especially attuned to evaluating the options carefully.

Is it possible to make a mistake in spite of careful deliberation? Sure. Sometimes a smart decision maker will even choose the second best option because of considerations within the environment. Suppose you believe, for instance, that choosing a particular supplier is the best option. Your boss, however, is really pushing for a different one. You need to consider how much political capital you want to spend fighting for your choice. Yes, you think your recommendation would be better. But would it be so much better that you would bet your relationship with the boss? Is it reasonable to consider your position within this context? Certainly.

Is there a point at which you might need to stick

to your recommendation in spite of the boss' agenda? Sure. What if it becomes apparent that supporting the boss' choice would be unethical or inappropriate? Then you need to ask your boss to take responsibility for the selection. If this creates an uncomfortable situation, at least you are maintaining your integrity.

Most substantial decisions involve other people, whether family, friends, or colleagues. Take, for example, a person you consulted about resolving an issue with a co-worker. This person has known the co-worker for a long time. You believe she would provide some accurate and relevant perspective. But then she tells you some information that seems to be based on hearsay or gossip. She also shares her opinions about the co-worker's kids and how they're always in trouble. Hmmm . . . that's not relevant. It might be better to approach someone who will provide you with verifiable information that does not appear to be biased.

The same thing can happen with information you find on-line. A search on any phrase these days will result in hundreds, if not thousands, of links. Most are not relevant. Many contain inaccurate, or perhaps distorted, information. It might be tempting to take what you find at face value. But it is better to verify for accuracy and relevance. The more critical the decision, the more important it is to do this.

The next variable in choosing the best option is importance. But importance to whom? If you are offered a job, for instance, the decision you make is more important to you than to the employer. It's not that they don't care, but you might be one of thousands on their payroll. To you, however, this firm will be your sole source of income. In some situations, the level of importance may be at the other end of the continuum. Deciding which restaurant to eat at might be one of these. How about choosing between reruns of *Survivor* or *Dancing with the Stars*? Then there's paper or plastic. Sorry, I let my mind wander.

DECISIONS THAT WILL HAVE A LASTING IMPACT

Answer two questions when making decisions that will have lasting impact: 1) How important is this decision to me? 2) How important is my decision to the people it will impact? Answering these two questions will provide you with valuable perspective on how to act.

I have served on the boards of a number of professional associations. An issue arising with each of these organizations has been the cost of membership. Some can get rather expensive. When this issue arises, I have to reflect on its importance from two perspectives. First, there's the importance to me. If I vote to increase dues, I'm taking more money out of my own pocket. Will I see increased value from the organization from an increase in dues?

Second, I need to look at the *importance* to other members and to the association itself. How is the organization's financial health? Are operating costs going up or are we mismanaging money? What will the members think? If they're not sold, we may lose a number of members. There are other considerations as well, but you get the picture. Reflecting on importance helps to frame the decision.

The final variable in choosing the best option is *emotion*. As with importance, the emotion associated with a decision can be placed on a sliding scale. Left or right in the parking lot? Who cares? Deciding which job to accept? That can really get you worked up.

This emotion may not be just yours. It can be the emotions of other people involved. After all, our emotions are wrapped up in everything. Have you ever, for instance, compared yourself to someone else and come out exactly even? It is human nature to consider ourselves better than or worse than those around us. Some of us are more sensitive to these emotions than others.

Sometimes my kids will say or do something silly. I will give them a disapproving look. They'll say, "Don't judge me!" in a playful sort of way. I tease them about being insecure. But think about it. We all feel insecure sometimes. This can be especially true when we're about to make a decision that doesn't feel right. Have you been there?

Even asking for help in a store can be unsettling. This is especially true if the clerk looks intimidating. If you see a scowl on his face, your first inclination might be to find someone else or simply surrender to searching on your own. You have to remember that the clerk's mood is *his* issue, not yours. After all, he's the clerk! Is this kind of feeling rational? Not really, but it certainly plays a role in the decisions we make. When you consider all three of these elements, information, importance, and emotion, you increase your chances of making a smart decision.

DECISIONS AND THE DESIRES OF OTHERS

Darla managed the training department of a pharmaceutical firm. She was responsible for selecting topics for each year's curriculum. She did this based on the surveys she received from managers throughout the firm. She tried to address everyone's needs. But a couple of the department managers constantly asked for additional training.

Darla had limited resources. She found herself caught between spreading this budget throughout all the departments and meeting the persistent demands of these two individuals. On one hand, she loved their enthusiasm. On the other, she wanted to focus on a couple of other departments. These had been neglected in the past and were experiencing high turnover and poor productivity.

When it came to information, Darla had more than enough since she had collected surveys and feedback from those she served. But the other two elements required more balance. In considering importance, she had to consider priorities. Since she had the broader perspective, she could see the needs of other departments conflicting with the requests of two eager managers. She recognized that unless she acted carefully someone was going to be disappointed. Then there was the emotional aspect. She did not want to disappoint anyone or let someone down. She also realized that some of her political capital would be on the line if she did not act with care and deliberation.

Darla sat down to consider her options: 1) She could take her budget and spread it evenly across all the departments. 2) She could focus on the two needy departments this year. Then she could focus on other departments in the future. This she would have to do in spite of her persistent colleagues. 3) She could look for other resources to augment her training budget.

In the end, she approached the two enthusiastic but persistent managers. She explained to them that she would be happy to address their needs. She insisted, however, that they would have to finance the training. Both readily agreed to do so. It turned out that both believed that training money was limited to what Darla had in her budget. When they approached senior management about using their own resources with Darla's assistance, their requests were granted. This example underscores why smart decision makers take time to ask lots of questions. They want to know whom their decision could impact. Leaping to conclusions with incomplete information can create all kinds of havoc.

We don't even think about most of the decisions we make every day. But there are some for which the stakes are higher. For these decisions, you have to take time to consider a variety of factors. These include the information and resources you have, the importance of the decision, and the emotion surrounding the situation. You can't just not act. So clarify the problem, collect your resources, consider your options, and choose the best option.

QUESTIONS TO CONSIDER

- Think back to a recent decision. What could you have done to improve the process for making it?
- Consider the three variables in all decisions – information, importance, emotion. What steps can you take to better consider these variables in making your everyday decisions?

REMEMBER to watch the video connected to this chapter by scanning the QR on the first page.

Reflect on what you've learned from each decision. If you don't cogitate on the outcome, you'll relearn it again down the road.

Thirteen

Cogitate on the Outcome

Cogitate is a whimsical word meaning "to reflect." In this impatient world it is easy to move on after making a decision without taking time to assimilate the result. Taking time to cogitate produces the little voice that sometimes yells, "Stop, this could be trouble!" when you are about to make a mistake. As these experiences build over time, smart decision makers develop a sixth sense about how to proceed in many situations.

Different generations cogitate differently. This is because of the way they learned to learn. If you're a digital immigrant, chances are you add these teaching moments to the experience you already have. The result, positive or less-than-positive, may have less impact simply because you are processing it through the lens of long experience.

If you're a digital native, chances are you are seeing it through the lens of your friends, colleagues, and the digital interactions that are so commonplace within your generation, a sort of collective knowledge so to speak. If this is your first experience with a type of decision, for instance, it will understandably have more of an impact on your psyche and emotions.

Those who make smart decisions do several things as they cogitate:

They take time to reflect. Smart decision makers stop and think. They interrupt the normal press of things to cogitate on what happened as a result of their decision. Was it the right action? Why? Why not? What could have been done better? What additional insights or information would have been helpful? You get the picture.

They embrace the value of peace and quiet. Inspiration and clarity seem to appear when the brain is not being bombarded with a constant media stream or parade in your office or at home?

They keep a log. This is not some fancy leatherbound book. It is a system that works best for them, like a memo app, an open document on a laptop, or a pad of paper on a bedside table.

They consult with others. Smart decision makers make a habit of asking others for feedback on what happened after a decision. What could have worked better? What have they learned? They encourage an environment of honest and open input.

* * *

I love the word *cogitate*. It simply means to reflect on or think about what you've learned. But just saying "cogitate" gives you a sense of whimsy. We all can use a little more of that.

In this impatient world, we're all trying to think at 4G speed. It can be easy to face a challenge, deal with it, live with the consequences, and move on without learning anything. Of course, if you don't learn anything, you risk repeating the same mistakes. Besides, accumulating knowledge allows you to anticipate future challenges and avoid bad decisions. Think about the last time you were about to take an action and then hesitated. The little voice in your head said, "Whoa! This could be trouble." Then you discovered that taking the action would have been a mistake. That's the result of cogitating on what you've learned. It probably felt satisfying, didn't it?

COGITATING GENERATIONS

The members of each generation approach cogitating differently. This is because of the time in which they came of age. If you're a digital immigrant (someone who came of age prior to menu-driven technology) chances are you'll cogitate based on your long experience. As with anyone, much of how you decide will be based on recent experiences. But a portion will be based on memories that were formed many years ago. All of this comes together when you take time to think about what you've learned from a particular situation.

If you're a digital native (someone who has come of age immersed in all the menu-driven technology), you've learned a different way to cogitate. This has made it easy for you to conclude that all answers must be available in a menu someplace. After all, music, entertainment, communication, travel, education, reading, and shopping all seem to be available by navigating through the menus on the device in your hand. If you believe the engineers and marketers, we will no longer have to think for ourselves after 2020. Of course, George Orwell was arguing the same thing in his novel *1984*, published in 1949.

But most of life's decisions don't work that way. This is especially true of relationships and career choices. If you've been relying on menu-driven applications, your brain is conditioned to expect options when making decisions. That's only natural. It develops connections and neural pathways based on what is reinforced. In simpler terms, you make decisions out of habit, just like everyone does. Through processes of elimination, for instance, you have discovered how to master new software. This is because its architecture uses the same construction that you learned by using other software.

Of course, mastering software is one thing. Learning to navigate the problems you face outside of menu-driven environments is quite another. This is why becoming overly reliant on digital menus can impair your ability to make decisions. (If you disagree with my argument here, I urge you to cogitate on what I'm saying before lashing out in an e-mail that begins with, "Hey you old fart! You're too old to understand today's digital wizardry.")

Pretty much every significant decision you make involves ambiguity. In other words, there's no completely right or wrong answer. Even pleasurable decisions such as buying a new car, taking a new job, or choosing a vacation spot involves some risk. You may not like the car after 30 days. You might discover your new boss is a bozo. It may rain throughout your vacation. All of this can produce a bit of stress and discomfort because of your fear of the unknown.

Can it be intimidating to make decisions where there's no definite answer? Sure, especially when there's no escape button to push. But we all have to start someplace and the sooner the better. There will always be people there to help when things don't go as planned. Some say that's what makes life interesting.

COGITATING AND SMART DECISION MAKERS

So, what do smart decision makers do to cogitate in a meaningful way? If you take time to observe them, here's what you'll see:

They take time to reflect. Smart decision makers stop and think. They get finished with an important meeting and step away from others to jot a few insights. They keep pads around the house so they never have to reach too far to record an idea. I know one writer who keeps a grease pencil in the shower so he can write on the walls when inspiration strikes. (His wife hates this!) The key is to interrupt the normal press of things to cogitate on what just happened. How many times have you tried to remember some bit of brilliance? Unfortunately, it lasted for a few seconds and then was flushed into oblivion by one distraction or another.

I met recently with a colleague about promoting this book, for instance. Over a period of two hours, he provided me with some great insights. Before I got into the car to drive home, I made sure to review our conversation in as much detail as I could. I did this for two reasons: 1) To open my mind to any new inspirations prompted by our conversation, and 2) To rehearse the details of what he said, better ensuring that what I had heard was encoded in my long-term memory. As you recall, the only information that makes it past the brain's short term (working) memory is information that remains a part of the brain's attention for more than three to five seconds. There's no way I captured everything he said. But I have a better chance of recalling the essentials when the need arises.

Smart decision makers embrace the value of peace and quiet. If aliens landed on earth, they might think that we're all afraid of silence. It's tough these days to find a public space that is not filled with entertainment or news. Some people argue that they think better with background noise. The latest brain research does not support this contention. Smart decision makers find places to get away from all the distractions and just listen. "Listen to what?" you might ask. The truth is they don't know in advance. But inspiration and clarity seem to appear when the constant media stream is not bombarding the brain. After all, who hasn't had a great idea in the shower, in the middle of the woods, or when the iPod's broken and there's nothing on the radio?

They keep a log. Sound like a pain? Not really. For most, this is not some fancy, leather-bound book. It's a spiral notepad. It's a document they keep open on their laptop or tablet. It's a memo app on their smart phone. It's an on-line application they can access from anywhere. What's key here is that smart decision makers jot notes, write down reflections, and record insights as they occur. With a working memory that lasts three to five seconds, you have to jot down ideas when they pop up.

They consult with others. Those who consistently make smart decisions recognize that those around them can provide valuable insights they had not considered. They make a habit of seeking input and discussing challenges before acting. Once they have made a decision, they will ask others for feedback on what happened. What improvements could have been made? What worked well? What have they learned? Over time, those around them understand that honest input is always welcome.

I meet with a group of colleagues every other month, for example, to exchange views and resources on a topic of mutual interest. Since we only have an hour, the discussion is always fast-paced. After each one of these meetings, I make it a practice of seeking out individuals who were in the room to ask what they learned. Without exception, they always share insights that didn't dawn on me in the meeting, even though I was there. Occasionally, someone will type up the notes he or she has taken and pass those along to others as well. All of this combines to provide each of us with multiple brains from which to learn.

So there you have them, the five Cs – Clarify, Collect, Consider, Choose, and Cogitate. Memorize this simple framework and you will have a built-in methodology for approaching and resolving the daily challenges that come your way. The best way to learn something is to apply it.

Lots of times, of course, we're faced with a problems for which there is no best answer. In the next chapter, we'll explore how those who make smart decisions deal with ambiguity.

QUESTIONS TO CONSIDER

- Think back to a recent experience where you had to make a significant decision. What did you learn from the experience?
- Read back through the characteristics outlined in this chapter. What steps can you take to better adopt them?
- Consider a decision you are currently facing. How can you better "cogitate" on the outcome after you have acted?

REMEMBER to watch the video connected to this chapter by scanning the QR on the first page.

Life is full of uncertainty. Comfort with ambiguity sets smart decision makers apart from everyone else.

Fourteen

Decisions and Ambiguity

Life is full of ambiguous situations. Ironically, the more rules we put in place, the more exceptions there seem to be. Each one of these exceptions requires you to deal with ambiguity. Other times, ambiguity is about relationships. Even if you've known the people involved for a long time, the outcome of what you decide may be unpredictable. Then there are the choices you make as a consumer, parent, employee, volunteer, voter, driver . . . you get the picture.

So how do smart decision makers deal with all these situations?

First, they take a step back and look at the big picture. We discussed this in Chapter Five. In a world filled with quick but inadequate answers, it is tempting to click the mouse, touch the screen, or press the button to get closure. But incorporating the big picture will give you the insights to make smarter decisions.

Second, they apply a problem solving process. Remember the 5Cs? When the pressure is on or the outcome is uncertain, it is tempting to act on the obvious solution. Smart decision makers possess the self-discipline to act methodically.

Third, they develop a comfort with ambiguity. Smart decision makers know that the outcome will not always be to their liking. But they anticipate this and work to mitigate any mistakes they make. They are more interested in making the smart decision than the popular or impatient one.

Life is full of ambiguous situations. How you deal with them determines how well you thrive in your surroundings. After all, that's what smart decision makers do all the time.

*   *   *

How do you go about making smart decisions in this ambiguous world? Ironically, the more we put rules in place to provide definite answers, the more exceptions seem to appear. Regardless of who you are or what you do, chances are your day is filled with situations requiring your judgment. So how do you deal with these issues in the midst of everything else? Here's what smart decisions makers do.

First, they take a step back and look at the big picture. We spent Chapter Five discussing this concept and I can't emphasize it enough. When you live in a world full of quick but inadequate answers, it is tempting to click the mouse, touch the screen, or scan your card to get to closure.

There's that momentary sense that you're done. As you know, however, you can end up with a shallow solution. The boss wants you to do it again, "the right way." The instructor returns the paper for a re-write. The team thinks you're cutting corners. Even though you accomplished the task, you get that nagging feeling that you could have, should have, done better.

Incorporating what you know about the big picture ensures that you get the best result possible. The big picture puts you inside the boss' head to better understand what she's looking for. The big picture provides you with the perspective needed to write a better paper. The big picture gives you the insights you need to really contribute to the team effort by adding that extra angle.

Second, smart decision makers apply a problemsolving process, such as the 5Cs, to the situation. (Remember? Clarify, Collect, Consider, Choose, Cogitate) When the pressure is on, when the stress is building, when the impatience is growing, when the outcome is uncertain, it's tempting to act on the most obvious solution.

A lot of today's impulsiveness is driven by all the instant answers that seem to offer easy solutions. "Want to re-finance? We can do it in three easy steps and less than 24 hours" (at unbearable interest rates). "Need a new career? Our people make a million dollars a year working from home" (and one of a million succeeds). "Want to become a social media expert? Watch this free seminar!" (which is really a 60 minute advertisement for the $1,000 package). Sorry. Do I sound skeptical here?

Those who make smart decisions act methodically. They know when to take their time and weigh all the possible options. They certainly feel the pressure to make impulsive decisions. But they resist the temptation. Like everyone, they've made mistakes. They have also learned from them. They know to pull back rather than act because of others' expectations. Some people complain about how slow these individuals can be in making a decision. But smart decision makers are more interested in making the smart decision than the popular or impatient one.

Third, individuals who make smart decisions have grown comfortable with ambiguity. They recognize uncomfortable situations as inevitable and methodically work to overcome them. They know that the outcome will not always be to their liking. But they work to mitigate the problem. Allowing a problem to overwhelm them is not an option. After all, if they don't act, the situation could get worse or they will have lost the opportunity.

They begin by taking a step back to examine the big picture. Next, they approach the problem methodically. Finally, they grow comfortable in coping with the inevitable ambiguous situations that confront everyone. Here's an illustration.

AMBIGUITY IN TUSCANY

Several years ago, a good friend of mine traveled with his wife to Bagnoregio, Italy, in the hill country of Tuscany. After spending a delightful day in the village, they missed the last bus back to where they were staying. There they were, in a small village that was going to sleep for the night. They spoke no Italian. They knew no one in town. There were no taxis. They felt totally alone. My friend kept saying to himself, "I love an adventure. I love an adventure," just to keep his mind off how stranded they were.

Standing on a street corner, they began to consider their situation methodically. First, they clarified the problem. They were stranded in a small Italian village without their luggage. They didn't speak the language. The sun was sinking below the horizon. Second, they collected their resources. They had credit cards. There had to be a room to rent someplace in this village. There had to be a store open so they could get something to eat. Surely, there were people who spoke English. They just had to find them.

Third, they considered their options. Who would speak English? The Police? Someone in a pharmacy? A travel agent? Fourth, they chose what appeared to be the best option and went looking for the police station. Unfortunately, no one there spoke a word of English and they were unceremoniously told to leave. Next, they went to the local pharmacy. The pharmacist was very nice, but spoke very little English and had no idea where they could spend the night. She did, however, point them toward a travel agency across the square. The travel agent, who spoke a bit of English, suggested they try a bed and breakfast in a house two blocks away. She wasn't sure if there would be any space, but it was worth a try.

The woman who answered the door at the bed and breakfast not only welcomed them, she spoke perfect English. She told her husband to call the hotel in the other town the couple came from to make sure their luggage wasn't discarded. Then she put them up in a beautiful room. On top of this, she introduced them to another couple from the United States and directed them all to a restaurant where the two couples spent three hours eating a wonderful meal.

Early the next morning, my friend and his wife took

the first bus back to where they were supposed to have stayed. As they rode through Tuscany's beautiful countryside, they cogitated on what they had learned from this unexpected adventure. While not the expected outcome, this couple came away from this experience none the worse for wear. They also have a great story to tell for a lifetime.

Life is full of ambiguous situations. How you deal with them determines how well you thrive in your surroundings. After all, that's what smart decision makers do all the time.

QUESTIONS TO CONSIDER

- Consider your emotions when faced with ambiguous situations or problems. What causes you discomfort?
- What coping strategies do you presently use to deal with these situations?
- Read back through the chapter. What one or two strategies would help you best deal with ambiguity?
- How can you best integrate these strategies into your everyday work and lifestyle?

REMEMBER to watch the video connected to this chapter by scanning the QR on the first page.

Think strategically. Take the long view. Seek frank input. Smart decision makers instill themselves with confidence.

Fifteen

Becoming a Smart Decision Maker

To smart decision makers, it is not enough to look at the big picture and use a framework for solving day-to-day problems. There are certain habits they have developed that guide their decision making. This means instilling within yourself the thought process of smart decision makers or, to coin a phrase, perform a *self-instill*. Here's what they do:

Smart decision makers embrace the big picture. This means they don't just know it's there, they actively investigate and immerse themselves in it.

They take the long view. They see the decisions they make as a part of a journey. They have learned from choices made in haste and take these experiences to heart.

They compartmentalize. Knowing that it takes from five to eighteen minutes to regain concentration after a distraction, smart decision makers work at getting away to concentrate on one thing at a time. They recognize the value of focus and clearly defined goals.

They think tactically. They recognize instances when a decision requires calculated consideration. They embrace a framework for problem solving, such as the 5Cs.

They seek differing opinions. Smart decision makers reach beyond their friends to obtain frank and honest feedback. They recognize that you need to ask the people affected by your decision to truly find out how it will be received.

They surround themselves with other smart decision makers. They form groups of like-minded people who are comfortable challenging each other's assumptions and decisions. These arguments make them sharper at identifying the best paths to pursue.

They delay gratification. Those who make consistently smart decisions have developed self-discipline. They resist jumping at the obvious answer. They do their homework. They embrace the value of perseverance.

All of this requires a change in mindset. To put it bluntly, we have become a society that seeks ease and comfort. We all also have a well-worn habit of rationalizing when things don't go our way. It seems like there's always someone else to blame or a silly rule that shouldn't apply to us. While there might be a few legitimate exceptions here, most of the time we're just unwilling to accept the consequences. I know, I've been guilty of this myself.

Those who make consistently smart decisions have developed the habits we just covered and continue to work at mastering them. How about you?

*　　*　　*

I have made a tradition of running the Bolder Boulder every year. Each Memorial Day, 50,000 people gather in Boulder, Colorado, to compete in this world-famous 10K. Over the years, I have watched with amusement as a few of those in each wave of runners race ahead the second the starter's pistol goes off. Not surprisingly, I pass many of these individuals one, two, or three miles into the event. While I'm no elite runner, I maintain a steady pace and finish well before most of those who throw all their energy into the first quarter mile.

I have reflected on how similar these behaviors can be to how people approach everyday problem solving. For some, the Bolder Boulder is all about getting finished, in spite of the pain and exhaustion. For others, it's taking time to enjoy the journey. For some, it's following the impulse to take off like a shot without regard to the overall challenge. For others, it's planning ahead by conserving energy for the long haul. For a few, it's simply about being in the moment and having fun. This includes the belly dancers, the individuals in gorilla costumes, and the people who walk the 6.2 miles backwards.

That begs the question, "What sets those who make consistently smart decisions apart from these rest of us?" They perform what I call a "self-instill." That's right, a self-instill. We've all become familiar with the concept of self-installs. Ordering cable? They send you a box to self-install. Purchasing new software? They will provide instructions on how to self-install. Given the state of health care, we may soon be self-installing body parts.

DEFINING A SELF-INSTILL

I'm talking about a *self-instill*. This means, instilling within yourself the thought process to be a smart decision maker. So what have those making smart decisions done to instill themselves with these essential characteristics? Routines. Do you have routines? I know I do. There's nothing like that cup of coffee in the morning or that weekly gathering of friends. In the midst of all the stress these days, it's comforting to have times when we can escape momentarily into something predictable.

The same might be said of work routines. There is a certain relief in knowing what's going to happen and how we're going to handle it every day. Sure, there's always room for a little excitement, just as long as it's not too off-the-wall or time consuming.

But as the saying goes, if you do what you've always done, you'll get what you've always gotten. For many, this is perfectly okay. Some however want to grow in what they do. To thrive like this, you have to think outside the box, color outside the lines, push the envelope, or alter the paradigm. Simply said, you have to *change*. Of course, the only people who enjoy change are wet babies. (Are you tired of the tacky sayings yet?)

Since you've gotten this far in the book, chances are you're willing to look at the big picture when dealing with problems. You'll be happy to use the 5Cs in dealing with the challenges you face. But you have to foster these strategies into routines. They have to become second nature. When problems arise you have to slide seamlessly into "figure-it-out" mode.

All of this requires a change in mindset. So if you aren't willing to change, and I mean for real, then smart decisions will continue to elude you. It can't be said any plainer. (If you want to abandon the book at this point, I understand.)

As you have probably discovered, we humans have a well-worn habit of rationalizing. The tougher the perceived challenge or change, the better we seem to be at finding ways to avoid taking action. We are assisted in this, many times, by the people around us. So let's talk about those issues for a minute.

To put it bluntly, we have become a society that seeks ease and comfort. Now there's nothing inherently wrong with this. Who doesn't want to enjoy the pleasures of life? We all know deep down, however, that achieving pleasure and comfort require time, effort and sacrifice. Walk up to random people on the street and ask, "Do pleasure and comfort require time, effort and sacrifice?" and most will say yes. (The rest are just fooling themselves.) Yet we are immersed in a sea of messages that preach convenience, pleasure, comfort, and entitlement all without time, effort, or sacrifice. But you don't thrive in life unless you're willing to put some "skin in the game." That means that good things come with your effort, time and willingness to change behaviors.

THE ELEMENTS OF A SELF-INSTILL

So how do those who make smart decisions get there when others don't? Watch them for a while and you will note the characteristics they display:

They embrace the big picture. We've spent a good deal of time talking about this in previous chapters. So I will refer you back to those for the insights you need. Just remember, people making smart decisions, make a habit of seeing the big picture in everything they do.

They take the long view. More than one philosopher has said that life is a journey, not a destination. Whether it's marriage, careers, hobbies, friendships, volunteer efforts, or anything else, those making smart decisions maintain perspective. The club to which you belong might be poorly led right now. Does that mean it's time to resign your twenty-year membership? Sure, you've gotten sideways with a good friend. Does that mean you should throw up your hands and end the relationship? Yes, you've been assigned a new project that you don't particularly enjoy. Is it worth putting up a fuss and spending your political capital on a short-term nuisance?

Those making smart decisions take the long view when making choices. Like anyone, they've made mistakes by acting in haste, acting emotionally, or even acting irrationally. But they take these experiences to heart and add them to their own long view.

They compartmentalize. In this distracting world, smart decision makers have mastered the skill of compartmentalizing their time. Again, this flies in the face of the talk about multitasking. But once you've settled into concentrating on something, doesn't it feel better to complete the task? Knowing that it takes up to 18 minutes to recover from distractions, these individuals plan time to focus on significant issues rather than just sit down someplace and try to think. As mentioned before, they hide someplace quiet. If you observe them,

you'll find that those consistently making smart decisions disappear periodically. Sometimes they reappear
after a couple of minutes. Sometimes they disappear
for longer. Sometimes they hang a "do not disturb"
sign on the door. Sometimes they take a walk, take a
hike, take a drive. In other words, whatever it takes.

They think tactically. In chapters Nine through
Thirteen, we talked about the 5Cs of problem solving.
This is an example of thinking tactically. Thinking tactically, as with looking at the big picture, is a learned
behavior.

"Are you telling me I need to think tactically when
doing something as simple as ordering a sandwich?"
you might ask. Well, yes and no. It depends on your
situation. That fourteen inch mega-juicy, super cheesy,
roast beef jumbo sandwich may hit the spot at noon.
You don't have to think tactically for a decision like
that. But will those 5000 calories put your lights out
during the important meeting at 2 PM? Asking that
simple question means you're thinking tactically. (I realize that the vegetarians reading this might be offend-
ed by my mention of roast beef. Sorry. Think tofu!)

How about situations that are more important
than sandwich selection? Ah, that's when it helps to
have developed a habit of being conscious of the present circumstances. I call it being situationally aware.
Let's consider a couple of examples.

Suppose you have been left alone staffing the hotel's

front desk. Business is slow. No one's within earshot. Do you: a) Catch up on Facebook? b) Download more songs to your smart phone? c) Wander around looking for someone to talk to? d) Organize the mess under the counter, restock all forms, clean the computer screens, and refill the printer paper? (Don't laugh, there are people out there who think this is a trick question.)

Here's another example. It's a busy afternoon. You've fallen behind on a project that's due tomorrow. Then a colleague texts you about an opportunity to meet someone who can have a positive impact on your career. What do you do? Do you act impulsively and jump at the chance? Do you stick to your project and kick yourself for missing the opportunity?

Perhaps you split the difference and break away from your work for a short while to visit with your colleagues. Then you excuse yourself by saying, "Pardon me for leaving, but I am up against a deadline and never like to be late with an assignment." Not only have you had a chance to connect with your colleagues, but also make a positive impression about your work ethic.

There are degrees of this of course. The key is to develop a sense of situational awareness. This will enable you to take better advantage of opportunities and avoid mistakes. As the musician was told when he asked how to get to Carnegie Hall, "practice, practice, practice."

They seek differing opinions. Smart decision makers also recognize that they tend to become who they hang around with. So with whom do you associate? I know, hanging out with people who think like you is easy. It's comforting. It's fun. You agree with each other.

But here's the thing. If everyone you hang around with thinks like you, you will continue to hear what you've always heard – same beliefs, same biases, same interests and . . . same ignorances. I'll be the first to agree that that's human nature. When it comes to many subjects, like sports, social activities, and so on, it's great to exchange views with like-minded people. Other times, the chips are down and the decisions have significance. You need to get outside the familiar circle for opinions and suggestions.

SEEK HONEST FEEDBACK

People who make smart decisions seek out people who are honest with their comments since they know that their advice will be sincerely considered. My friend, Ed Oakley, co-wrote a great book titled *Enlightened Leadership*. He could have just gone with his favorite title. He could have passed it around among his friends to get their blessings and then gone to press. Instead, he and his co-author headed to the airport. They spent several hours approaching travelers dressed in business attire since they would be their target audience. They showed each of them a selection of possible titles and let them comment on which they found most intriguing. There are now more than 300,000 copies of *Enlightened Leadership* in print, partly because of their willingness to seek out differing opinions. How can you apply this strategy?

Smart Decision Makers surround themselves with other smart decision makers. Don't you feel affirmed when people you respect agree with your decision? Even when it doesn't work out the way you hoped, you can take comfort that similar minds would have done the same thing. Just as those who make smart decisions look for differing opinions, they also seek support and energy from those facing similar challenges.

Some form groups of like-minded people and meet with them regularly. Sometimes called "masterminds" or "expert groups," they provide the participants with the opportunity to discuss challenges, dilemmas, significant decisions, and so on. You can receive some brilliant insights from those around you. You might also share just what someone else needed to hear.

The key is to reach out to those who you have observed making smart decisions. Not all will have the time or interest. Not all will turn out to be as good at decision making as you thought. But with perseverance, you'll be able to develop a group you can rely on.

Smart Decision Makers delay gratification. Those who consistently make smart decisions have developed self-discipline. They resist jumping at the obvious answer, the emotional option or the pressured choice. More than anything else, they have developed a sense that good things come to those who have patience.

Let's talk about this concept for a second. In 1970, Stanford professor Walter Mischel conducted a study that became known as The Marshmallow Experiment. In it, he sat young children (ages 4-6) by themselves in an empty room and then presented them with a marshmallow and a promise that if they didn't eat it until he returned (about 15 minutes later) he would give them a second one. As you might imagine, some kids ate the marshmallow the minute he left the room. The majority, however, resisted eating it for a number of minutes. A few kids resisted eating it until Dr. Mischel returned. Follow-up studies over the next thirty years revealed that those who were able to resist eating the marshmallow for longer periods of time tended to have better life outcomes, such as higher SAT scores, educational attainment, and other measures.

Those who choose to delay their decisions until the big picture has been considered and the choices are clear are generally rewarded with better outcomes, regardless of the endeavor. Everyone is continually tempted in this demanding, impatient, and impulsive world. So what separates those who make smart decisions from those who don't? It is their discipline to resist instant gratification. They know how to deal with artificial and unreasonable demands. They come to a methodical conclusion as to how to act. Then they do.

One of the positive results of instilling good habits is that important decisions become easier to make. When you have the information, discipline, and perspective, even risky decisions become calculated. Let's talk about that next.

QUESTIONS TO CONSIDER

- What is the most positive habit or routine you have? (If you can't think of one, what's the one you would like to have?)
- What are the elements, experiences, or advice that contributed most to developing this habit?
- What strategy can you use to build another of these habits?
- Pick one habit and write a declarative statement describing it. (For instance: In the next 30 days, I will establish a habit of using the 5Cs problem solving framework to make better decisions. I will accomplish this by applying the 5Cs to at least one decision I face everyday.)

REMEMBER to watch the video connected to this chapter by scanning the QR on the first page.

Calculated risk is all about confidence, understanding the big picture, and using a reliable solid problem-solving strategy. Do you?

Sixteen

Smart Decisions and Calculated Risk

Making smart decisions is all about taking calculated risks. This means you've considered the big picture and run your problem through a framework that clarifies the issue. But these two elements are not enough. You need to acknowledge the role that confidence plays in decisions large and small.

Consider the self-perceptions you live with every day. Some psychologists call them scripts. Perhaps you grew up hearing, "You're no good at math" or "Life is tough and then you die." Maybe you've been told, "You can relate to anyone" or "You've always been a strategic thinker." These scripts have an impact on our relationships with others, our perceptions of self-worth, and a host of other elements.

These messages have an impact on our confidence and, in turn, on our decisions. In a very personal way, they will influence whether you accept the job offer, buy the fancy car, or date the cute co-worker. These scripts can also influence the decisions you make on the job, as a volunteer leader, and in many other settings.

Any decision of consequence involves an element of calculated risk. If you have a clear perception of what you need to do, but not the confidence to do it, you can harm both yourself and others. Those making consistently smart decisions understand the role personal confidence plays in these equations and work to maintain their mettle even when fearful thoughts invade their attention.

Calculated risks all come down to the question, "What are the chances?" Understanding and accepting these chances enable smart decision makers to move forward confidently.

*   *   *

I jump out of perfectly good airplanes. How about you? There's nothing like falling face down at 120 miles per hour gazing out at the sky and landscape around you through a rush of wind. Then you open your parachute and float gently to the ground ready to do it again.

Maybe skydiving is not your thing. But we all take risks, large and small. The key is being as informed as possible before taking action. In other words, those who make smart decisions take calculated risks.

CONFIDENCE AND SMART DECISIONS

Calculated risks involve the two elements we have been spending a good deal of time discussing – looking at the big picture and using a methodology for solving problems (such as the 5Cs). But there's a third element that's essential to calculated risk-taking. That's confidence as a result of experience. Consider the areas of your life where you possess confidence. Then think about the areas where you don't. You might, for instance, be very comfortable approaching strangers. No matter what the situation, you're confident in your ability to relate. On the other hand, mathematics may intimidate the heck out of you. You might even have a little voice in your head that repeats, "I'm lousy at math," every time you're asked to multiply something. Both of these beliefs are the result of experience.

Chances are, you've had a lot of practice approaching strangers. It's fun. So you naturally look for environments where you can meet new people. Perhaps you were influenced by parents who said, "You can talk to anyone. You're great at relating to others."

On the other hand, those same parents may have said, "Math is so hard. Nobody in our family has ever been good at it." Perhaps you struggled early on with some basic math and just naturally avoid it whenever possible. For this reason, you've probably had very little practice and lack the confidence to get better.

Those who make smart decisions recognize that they're not going to be good at everything. But they also realize that there will be skills they need to develop in order to thrive. So they take all of this into consideration and look at unfamiliar challenges through three lenses:

First, they consider the *big picture*. In other words, what factors are going to impact this decision? Second, they consider what *resources* are available? What options are possible? What is the option with the most likelihood of success? Third, they consider the *chances* of failure versus the chances of success? This is where the calculation comes in. If they've been in a similar situation before, that experience informs them. If it went well, then they are more confident that there is a comfortable level of risk with this one. If they have not been in a similar situation, they will rely more on what they know to calculate the risk involved. Calculated risks all come down to the question, "What are the chances?" Regardless of the situation, those making smart decisions have instilled within themselves a methodology for calculating risks.

Of course, this still does not make it any easier when you're on the verge of doing something permanent. Sometimes the toughest part of making a smart decision is just making it. A while back I discovered a water leak behind the wall in an upstairs bathroom. This kind of leak can be the most maddening because you know it's there, but you don't know it's exact location. While you can grumble all you want, it needs to be repaired, and fast. This involves cutting into a perfectly good wall in order to find the leak, fixing the problem and then re-pairing the wall. When it is in the shower, this can mean breaking through tile, which is expensive and messy.

When I discovered the leak, it took me more than a day to act for the very reason I just described. No one wants to break into a perfectly good wall. Then, I be-gan to evaluate the situation in a calculated way. How bad could it be? What's the most it would cost? How much time could it possibly take?

"So what happened?" you might ask. Luckily, the other side of this wall was in a bedroom. So rather than destroying the tile wall in the shower, I was able to cut into the drywall behind a dresser. The problem turned out to be a pinhole leak in an old copper pipe that had simply developed over a very long time. It took me 15 minutes to patch the hole in the pipe and a total of one hour over the next couple of days to repair the wall.

Like anyone else, I had let my mind run away to the worst case scenario.

The bottom line? When you know what to do, don't stew. Gather the information you need. Consider your options. Choose the best option and attack the situation. As the old saying goes, "Beginning is half done."

So there you have it. Those who make smart decisions develop the habits of looking at the big picture and adhering to a methodology for solving problems. They take the long view and learn to think tactically. They seek out differing opinions and surround themselves with other smart decision makers. They delay their desire for instant gratification. Finally, they grow comfortable with taking calculated risks.

All that may sound like a lot to accomplish, especially when the world around you is preaching ease, impatience, convenience, and entitlement. But mastered with practice and perseverance, you too can become a smart decision maker in this dumbed-down world.

QUESTIONS TO CONSIDER

- How have the scripts in your head impacted the life decisions you have made?
- What was the last consciously calculated risk you took? What did you learn about your comfort in making decisions?

- What is the one action or strategy you can commit to so you'll feel more comfortable taking calculated risks?

REMEMBER to watch the video connected to this chapter by scanning the QR on the first page.

Decisions that affect you happen whether or not you participate. So why not take the time to "figure it out?!"

Seventeen

Figure It Out!

If you've made it this far, chances are you have become a smarter decision maker already. We all make a continuous series of decisions every day. But some have more significance than others. Sure, it's easy to fly through choices about what to wear, what to eat, or what to watch.

Then there are the decisions that can make a difference in your life, your career, your relationships. Smart decision makers instinctively know to take a step back and consider consequences, resources, relationships, and other elements.

Everyone drops the ball at times. No one is perfect. But smart decision makers maintain their focus, learn from the outcome, and make the necessary adjustments.

The big key is that they take action even when it requires calculated risk. Remember, decisions that affect you happen whether or not you participate.

On one hand, you can follow the crowd. You can take the advice of others because it's easy, simple, or non-confrontational. You can explain away the reasons why decisions didn't go your way. On the other hand, you can embrace the big picture. You can hone your problem solving skills. You can self-instill the characteristics of smart decision makers. When you do, you'll be able to say with confidence, "I figured it out!"

*   *   *

Everybody becomes a product of the times in which they come of age. Think about what that means for you. If you were born prior to the digital age, you learned to do most things manually. Need a new shirt? Drive to the store. Don't know the definition of a word? Locate a dictionary and look it up. Need to send someone a document? Drop it in a mailbox. Some of us even had to walk all the way to the television to change the channel.

If you've come of age in the past twenty years, much of what you've learned to do can be accomplished without leaving your chair. In fact, a tremendous amount of the work you need to do doesn't have to be done anymore. Is this good or bad? Neither. It's just different.

What does all this have to do with decisions? *Everything!* Much of decision making is based on your assumptions. Your assumptions are based on experience, observations,, and what someone else tells you. If you think about it, these assumptions determine the outcome in much of our daily lives. Some of this is conscious. Most of it is unconscious.

We all navigate our way through everyday life making a continuous series of decisions. From the time we get up in the morning until the time we go to sleep, there are probably hundreds of them. Most are routine. What should you wear? Which way should you drive to work? Would you like fries with that?

Then you face the decisions that are more crucial. Should you accept the job? Should you buy a new or used car? Should you enroll in that new training program? Some are work-related, others are personal. These decisions require more contemplation and more patience. They must be made in the context of other people and priorities. The outcome depends on the time and methodology you put into the considerations.

Think back to your last decision of consequence. Did you really take the time to deliberate before taking action? I know. There are times when I forget as well. Or maybe I was lazy, impatient, stressed, or one of those other emotions that plague all of us occasionally.

Those who make smart decisions drop the ball at times too. No one is perfect. But here's the thing, they work at maintaining their focus. They take the long view and understand that today's decisions can have considerable impact a long way down the road. Whether it's a personal issue or something at work, they've developed a habit of stepping back when they recognize that the outcome of the situation could impact them in more than a short-term way.

Here's something to consider. Decisions that affect you happen whether or not you participate. Let me repeat that. Decisions that affect you happen whether or not you participate.

You decided to read this book to become a better decision maker. As I've said before, you're fighting an uphill battle with the surrounding temptations. You could give in to those distractions. You could follow the crowd. You could go along with whatever is programmed into the computerized menus. You could simply do whatever you're told and that's it.

Or you can take the long view. You can look at the big picture. You can adopt a method for solving problems. You can surround yourself with other smart decision makers. You can instill in yourself the situational awareness and a confident orientation toward calculated risk. Does this take time? Yes. Will the people around you wonder what's going on as you change your mindset? Sometimes. Will you begin to embrace a new confidence in your ability to make smarter decisions in spite of the endless distractions and bits of shallow advice? Absolutely. The choice is yours. Just figure it out!

QUESTIONS TO CONSIDER

- What is the one recent decision that was made for you because you failed to take timely action?
- What would you do differently if that decision was still available to make?
- Congratulations! You've read the entire book. What is the one action you can take in the next day to turn these principles into action? (There's no time like the present.)

REMEMBER to watch the video connected to this chapter by scanning the QR on the first page.

ACKNOWLEDGMENTS

The inspiration for this book has come from count-less people – friends, clients, colleagues, even strangers – who said just the right things when I needed to hear them. It has been a labor of love, assembling all the stories and ideas from the past 25 years of working with employ-ers, educators, and parents.

Then there are those special "collaborators" who have contributed ideas, moral support, and even kicks in the butt to get all this into a book. It's always impos-sible to remember and name everyone. But a special shout goes to Marjii Middleton, my long-time assistant and foil. All that behind-the-scenes stuff she does has allowed me to focus.

Then there are my colleagues within the National Speakers Association. All have helped me think through the concepts in this book, challenge my assumptions, proffer clarity, and provide reassurance that this book really is a meaningful contribution. Special kudos go to Greg Godek and Orvel Ray Wilson for their expertise.

Then there are Erin and Katie who are first, two wonderful daughters, and second my very own in-house digital natives. You mean more to me than you'll ever know.

Finally, I want to thank Wendy, the love of my life, my soul mate, and my best friend. Your endless patience, tolerance, inspiration, insight, sense of humor and support continue to propel me through this long journey. Wow!

INDEX

ABOUT THE AUTHOR

Bob Wendover teaches organizations how to help their people make better decisions. A popular speaker, he is the author of nine books, including *Crossing the Generational Divide* and *Smart Hiring*. His weekly blog, *Common Sense by Friday*, features interviews and insights with smart decision makers who are making a difference.

Reach him at bob@bobwendover.com

This book is available at special quantity discounts to use as premiums and sales promotions or for use in corporate training programs. To obtain additional information, please e-mail us at: bulksales@articulatepublications.com.

CPSIA information can be obtained at www.ICGtesting.com
Printed in the USA
BVOW08s1859160516

448297BV00001B/9/P